Understanding and Counseling THE SUICIDAL PERSON

Paul W. Pretzel

Nashville   **ABINGDON**   New York

UNDERSTANDING AND COUNSELING THE SUICIDAL PERSON

Copyright © 1972 by Abingdon Press

ISBN 0-687-42802-5

Library of Congress catalog card number: 70-185553

MANUFACTURED BY THE PARTHENON PRESS AT
NASHVILLE, TENNESSEE, UNITED STATES OF AMERICA

Dedicated
in love
to my four favorite people
Anna Marie
Cynthia
Kathryn
Linda

Foreword

Here is a book which derives its usefulness from Paul Pretzel's knowledge of research findings on suicide, his experience in counseling with suicidal persons and their families, and his dual training in the theological and psychosocial disciplines. I am pleased to have an opportunity to affirm its usefulness and to commend it to those who desire to increase their understanding and ability to help persons facing this widespread human problem.

To those of us in the counseling professions, the issue of suicide is one of inescapable concern. The threat of self-destruction on the part of a client, parishioner, or patient arouses a wide range of feelings in the counselor. To be maximally effective in counseling with suicidal persons, it is essential to identify and work through our own feelings about suicide. This book, with its case illustrations and its frank discussion of the complex facets of the problem, can be a stimulus and a resource in this aspect of our growth as professionals.

Suicide and the threat of suicide confront the counselor and the counselee with life-death issues which our culture prefers to ignore. Because the problem involves us in struggling with the very fabric and meaning of human existence, it raises problems which are at once theological and psychological. In the swirling turmoil of the suicidal person's inner world, grasping for personal worth and meaning is interwoven with interpersonal conflicts and societal pressures. An effective approach to helping such a person must involve understandings and methods which deal with these multiple dimensions.

The special strength of the book is at this point. The author's understanding of the dynamics of religion in the problem is balanced by his insights concerning the psychosocial aspects of understanding and counseling the suicidal person. The unique contribution of the book to the tools of the counseling professions is derived from this dual competency.

The counseling art is most effective when techniques are based on a solid foundation of understanding of persons, their problems, and their potentialities. This volume is an example of such understanding-based methodology. The author undergirds his discussion of counseling and preventive methods by presenting the relevant facts from the science of suicidology. His approach illustrates the importance and usefulness of such facts in evaluating, e.g., the probable degree of lethality in a particular person's suicide threat. Yet the author's awareness of the unique and private hell of each individual is not obscured by his interest in knowledge regarding the general problem.

One of the valuable parts of the book for me is the discussion of the six levels of intervention in the suicidal situation. What one does in attempting to help depends on the stage, lethality, and particular circumstances in a given situation. Paul Pretzel's insights about how the helping person decides on appropriate intervention will be useful to those on the front lines in working with troubled people.

For clergymen and lay persons who deal with family members after a suicide has occurred, knowledge of how to facilitate their recovery from an infected grief wound is essential. The chapter on helping the survivors takes full account of the fact that recovery is more difficult at every stage than in a typical nonsuicide related grief experience.

The section of the book which explores the religious foundations of current attitudes toward suicide and ethical issues related to suicide exposes the reader to some often-ignored but crucial philosophical dilemmas, not the least of which is whether all suicides *should* be prevented. This discussion helps one define and refine his own ethical-philosophical presuppositions regarding suicide. Unless this happens, the counselor's presuppositions can distort his relationships with suicidal persons and their families.

The fact that Paul Pretzel has taken the spiritual-philosophical-existential dimension of the problem seriously increases the book's importance to both clergymen and to those in the secular counseling disciplines. It can be useful to clergymen in sharpening their ability to make their special contribution as theologically trained counselors. For those in the mental health professions, it can serve to enhance awareness of the vertical dimension in all human problems—the dimension of meaning and of "at homeness" in the universe—which goes beyond psycho-social categories and therapies.

In discussing the spiritual-philosophical dimension, the author goes to the heart of the religious issue—the experience of basic trust. He emphasizes leading the suicidal person to affirm something of value and helping him establish a nurturing relationship to strengthen his basic trust. These thrusts are vital for the continuing therapy following the acute crisis.

In addition to its obvious value for professional counselors, the book is a practical resource for training lay befrienders and crisis counselors (in both church and mental health settings). Its clear, unwordy approach to both understanding and helping suicidal persons makes it useful for anyone who wants to know more about the problem or who is confronted by it in his everyday relationships.

Exploration of the subject of suicide can provide a window into many aspects of the basic human predicament, illuminating much wider areas than the problem itself. By combining clinical competence, psychodynamic sophistication, and the theological understanding of a pastoral counselor, Paul Pretzel has opened such a window with this book.

Howard J. Clinebell, Jr.

Foreword

Death is one of the most pervasive taboo areas of our time. Since recorded time it has been denied, disguised, rejected, and feared. It is only relatively recently that progress has been made in overcoming these feelings, at least to the extent that it has entered more readily into the realm of open social discourse and close professional consideration. Books have appeared, articles have been written and institutes have been established to stimulate explorations and investigations into this "dark side of life." Of all the forms of death, suicide has met with most resistance, probably because the act itself has such forceful implications of total rejection for those left behind. It says much more in addition, for it both confesses and accuses, arousing feelings with which most survivors have great difficulty.

It is exactly in this area of confused feelings that Dr. Pretzel's writings have their greatest value. Throughout each chapter is the plea for understanding—of the act, the actor, the survivors, and the helpers. In this increased understanding lies the hope that the number of lives saved can be increased and the tragedies of unnecessary, premature death avoided.

Dr. Pretzel aims for increased understanding through

education, information, and training. The extent of his experience in working with suicidal patients and their families is readily apparent in the concrete, practical advice he provides. He tells how to help the panicky person who has reached the twin points of hopelessness and helplessness, and is desperately searching for an understanding and accepting ear. One has to recognize (respond), evaluate (determine lethality), intervene (restore hope), and follow through (keep communication channels open). It isn't easy as anyone who has worked with suicidal people can attest, because they are often filled with an insatiable need for the caring they lack. Often those first contacts with the concerned helper begin the vital task of building the trust so basic for survival and self-esteem.

What is needed then is tolerance, acceptance, and a willingness to become involved. But this is possible only when the helper is able to understand his own frustrations and to come to terms with his own aspirations. It also means facing his own feelings about death. Man does not easily come to terms with his own mortality and the flaunting disregard of the value of life by the suicidal person arouses many feelings which can impede both the availability and quality of help.

One way to relieve some of the feelings around suicide is to see it in proper historical perspective, to recognize its pervasiveness and ubiquity. Seeing suicide in its various settings as it was influenced by the specific cultures gives one a deeper understanding of the role in social and individual affairs. Feelings about suicide have not always been what they are today. Within the same culture suicide has been both condemned and condoned, depending apparently on the presence or absence of reason, individualism, authoritarianism, and other societal factors. Man's own tendencies to depression have always existed, of course, but his expression of these feelings through self-destruction has varied depending on the social and moral vectors of his time.

With increased understanding comes greater opportunity to provide help effectively. Dr. Pretzel writes for clergymen, physicians, and police, who are the most important of the frontline gatekeeper personnel in mental health. Clergymen have an unparalleled opportunity for help in this area. Their counsel is sought not only before the crisis, but also in the post-crisis, either for the suicidal person if he lives, or for the survivors if he does not. They are trusted and respected, basic human attitudes they not only receive but give, and these are attitudes which are most necessary and helpful for the suicidal person who has become convinced of his worthlessness. No one (other than an original parent) has more possibility of providing by precept the fundamental tenets for mental health, such as love, respect, appreciation, reasoned firmness, and readily available concern. The clergyman represents the acceptance of the community and the security of the spirit. He is needed to understand and to counsel. This book should help make his task easier.

Norman L. Farberow

Preface

The production of any book, it now seems to me, calls for about equal parts of determination and presumption. The question of determination is the author's own problem, whereas the amount of presumption he musters directly affects many other people. He must presume that he understands the person on whose behalf he is speaking (in this case the suicidal person) well enough to say something significant about him to a group of people whom he presumes will read what he has written to learn something new.

In addition, he must be presumptuous enough to sign his name to ideas and conceptions that were originally developed and researched by many other people. The whole idea for this book as well as the doctoral dissertation which preceded it, came from heavy reliance on two important institutions in the Los Angeles area, The School of Theology at Claremont, and the Los Angeles Suicide Prevention Center.

Any reader familiar with the Los Angeles Suicide Prevention Center will easily recognize the great debt owing. My first contact with the center was with its cofounder and then codirector, Edwin S. Shneidman, Ph.D. His interest in me and in the area of suicide and religion provided needed support and direction at a time when I had some interest but no clear idea of how one goes about conducting research into such an area. It was also because of Dr. Shneidman's continuing interest that I was later able to join the staff of the center first in the capacity as pastoral counselor and later as staff psychologist and codirector of clinical services.

A further debt is owed to the center's other cofounder and codirector, Norman L. Farberow, Ph.D., who has kindly consented to write a foreword for this volume. Dr. Farberow's interest in philosophy and religion as well as his open attitude to developing new styles of suicide prevention was an important stimulus to me. It was through Dr. Farberow's encouragement that I began to develop the presumption to publish.

One of the richest memories I have of my six years with the center is that of the weekly case conference, usually conducted by the clinical director, Robert E. Litman, M.D. The entire staff participated by presenting case material for discussion and analysis. Dr. Litman provided the basic theoretical framework for these discussions and was mainly responsible for making them the valuable learning situations that I found them to be. Norman D. Tabachnick, M.D., the associate chief psychiatrist at that time, provided a combination of clinical experience and literary interest that added a unique dimension to the whole atmosphere of the center.

The professional staff of the center functioned smoothly as a highly effective therapeutic team capable of creative and inventive responses to difficult and dangerous situations. Especially significant to me were the other psychologists on the staff, Carl I. Wold, Ph.D., who was my supervisor when the field was new to me, and Michael L. Peck, Ph.D., with whom I spent many valuable hours providing professional workshops for school counselors and teachers in the area of crisis intervention for adolescents. The motion picture we made together for the Los Angeles County School Superintendent is still in use.

Sam M. Heilig, M.S.W., and David J. Klugman, M.S.W., were the cochief social workers of the center. Their generosity in sharing their many years of clinical experience with suicidal persons make them important contributors to this book. My gratitude to these close friends is deep.

Another group who provided me with more than they know is the large group of nonprofessional volunteers whom I was privileged to train and supervise. Dedicated and concerned lay people, they represent the large number of good persons in any community who willingly give up much of their time and pleasure to other people who need help. The center could not have functioned clinically without them, and I am sure they are aware of my feelings of affection and gratitude for them.

The School of Theology at Claremont is the second institution that played a major role in the production of this volume. Howard J. Clinebell, Ph.D., is especially important to me, having served as my major advisor and chairman of my dissertation committee. Dr. Clinebell made many important contributions to the whole development of my thinking and interests. I am indebted to him again for his willingness to contribute one of the forewords to this book.

David D. Eitzen, Ph.D., deserves a special word of thanks for his help at several crucial points.

The typing of the manuscript was a difficult job that

was shared at one time or another by the entire secretarial staff of the Suicide Prevention Center. It was Mrs. Alice Arnold, however, who carried the bulk of the work and to her I am especially grateful. Mrs. Winifred Bock made the difficult task of revision surprisingly smooth and easy, and my thanks go to her.

Finally, a word of gratitude must go to all my own patients, and to all the patients of the Suicide Prevention Center. My hope is that their despair and suffering may through this book be the grounds for help for others.

Paul W. Pretzel

Contents

Introduction

Fifty-seven-year-old Dr. Murphy sat alone in his darkened office. It was late at night. He was partly drunk. Twenty-seven years of successful medical practice, four children, a host of friends: These were the plus marks. A painful divorce four years ago, two quick unhappy marriages, a slowly increasing alcohol problem, increasing doubts about his own professional competency, a summons to appear in court next week on a drunk driving charge—his fourth, certainly loss of license and perhaps jail: These were the minus marks.

Dr. Murphy carefully took a bottle of barbiturates from the medicine cabinet and swallowed the contents. He was found dead the next morning.

The suicide rate in the United States maintained itself, in recent years, at about the level of 11.0. This means that every year, out of every one hundred thousand of the general population, eleven people will kill themselves. Another way of expressing this is that one percent of all deaths are suicide. For every person who dies by suicide, there are probably about fifteen who are making suicide attempts.

These figures are based on reports submitted by coroners'

offices from every county in the union and represent only those deaths that have been formally certified as suicide. How many actual suicides have been improperly certified as either accidental or natural death, of course, no one knows. Some estimates say the suicide rate is actually double the reported rate. Sometimes families will destroy suicide notes to avoid the stigma of having a suicidal death in the family, and family physicians have been known to certify a death falsely for the same reason. County coroners occasionally fail to investigage deaths sufficiently to discover hidden suicide.

Many of the twenty-five thousand Americans who kill themselves each year are, like Dr. Murphy, valuable contributing members of their communities whose lives affect hundreds of others. Many of their tragic and untimely deaths could be prevented if others in the community better understood the nature of suicidal depression and despair.

Karl Menninger dramatizes the urgency of the problem: "Once every minute or even more often, someone in the United States either kills himself or tries to kill himself with conscious intent. Sixty or seventy times everyday these attempts succeed. In many instances they could have been prevented by some of the rest of us." [1]

Suicide is the tenth highest cause of death in the United States; more deaths occur by suicide than by murder, and in Los Angeles County, more people die from suicide than traffic accidents. It would be difficult to exaggerate the seriousness of the problem.

In recent decades the subject of suicide has been receiv-

[1] Menninger, Foreword to *Clues to Suicide,* Edwin S. Shneidman and Norman L. Farberow, eds. (New York: McGraw Hill, 1957) , p. vii.

ing increased attention. We now know more about the sociology and psychology of suicide than ever before as the result of ever-increasing research being conducted into different aspects of suicide. Suicide prevention activities are more intensive than at any other time. This increased activity and knowledge has come about because the scientific community has recognized the problem as serious and has taken the mantle of responsibility for increased knowledge and action.

Beginning in the nineteenth century, the scientific inquiry into suicide began with empirical studies and the accumulation of data. The intent was to gain as much information as possible in order to understand the circumstances surrounding suicidal behavior. There are two broad facets of this scientific endeavor, the sociological and the psychological. Sociology studies the social patterns and the social relationships surrounding persons in order to understand the social factors that contribute to suicide. The psychological approach attempts to understand the intrapsychic structure and the dynamics of the suicidal person. This volume will investigate the problem of suicide from both of these disciplines. But suicide is more than a scientific puzzle. It is a human problem, and therefore a religious problem.

When William James was in his mid-twenties, living in Europe, he suffered a severe depression marked with strong suicidal tendencies. He was alone, depressed, in an alien country, and struggling with the question of whether or not life was worth living. This was no academic question for him; he was deciding whether or not to kill himself.

Years later, in an address to the Harvard YMCA, speaking on the basis of his personal experience, he considered how he would respond to someone who was seriously considering suicide. "Let me say, immediately, that my final appeal is to nothing more recondite than religious faith. . . . Pessimism is a religious disease, it consists of nothing more than a religious demand to which there comes no normal religious reply." [2]

James was not offering religious faith in terms of trite moralisms or a rigid adherence to a system of dogma. He was speaking of religious faith in terms of "a healthy ultimate relationship with the universe." He was speaking in terms of man's basic religious need for a sense of meaning, purpose, and commitment in his life. He was speaking of faith in an "unseen order" in life, which gives us the ability to maintain our inner stability when the evils and stresses of the world seem ready to overcome.

Suicide is a religious problem because it involves man. It is a religious problem because it deals with ultimate things: life and death, good and evil, meaning and despair, and these are the time-honored concerns of religion.

In addition to being a subject of intense theological interest, suicide has also been the subject of considerable philosophic thought. The philosophical approach to the subject of suicide, beginning with the early Greek philosophers, attempts to incorporate the suicidal act into an overall consistent cosmology. Suicide is usually discussed from a judgmental viewpoint; that is, either the person does or does not have the right to kill himself. Suicidal behavior is moral or immoral, bad or good.

Attempts to prevent suicide in the philosophic and re-

[2] William James, *The Will to Believe and Other Essays in Popular Philosophy* (New York: Longmans Green, [1897] 1904) , p. 39.

ligious traditions included such techniques as the authoritarian prohibition of the right to commit suicide, condemnation of the act as sinful or immoral, threats of everlasting punishment, reprisals against the family of the suicide, abuse of the corpse of the suicide, and compulsory
forfeiture of certain legal and religious privileges and rights.
With the advent of the scientific emphasis in understanding
causes of the phenomenon, the methods of suicide prevention changed. The emphasis was now placed on improving social conditions so that some of the stresses which had
been seen as encouraging suicidal behavior might be eliminated or substantially reduced. In addition, agencies sprang
into existence with the purpose of coming to the aid of the
individual person who evidenced a likelihood of being
suicidal. Suicide was seen as a "cry for help."

But only a small proportion of suicidal people call an
agency. Most are lost somewhere in the general population
not knowing where to turn or how to deal with their intensive, overwhelming feelings. If they are to be helped it will
be because some nonprofessional person was sensitive to
their plight, heard their distress and knew how to make an
appropriate response.

This volume is written in the hope that increased awareness of the sociology and the psychology of suicide, as well
as better understanding of the philosophical and theological
issues involved will result in more effective suicide prevention.

Chapter 1
People Who Kill Themselves

The question of why people kill themselves is a highly complex and complicated matter. Suicidal motivations differ widely from situation to situation, making any generalizations of limited helpfulness. Depression, feelings of hopelessness, guilt, and shame are certainly common among suicidal persons, and these feelings usually arise in response to specific stress. Some of the most common of these stresses are the experience of important losses, such as the death or divorce of a loved one; failures on the job or in school, exposure of secret behaviors, like heterosexual affairs or a homosexual liaison; or a breaking through the barrier of consciousness by unacceptable thoughts and fantasies which produce feelings of fear and shame. Perhaps it would be helpful to meet some people who felt driven to the point of suicide.

DR. MURPHY

Dr. Murphy is representative in many ways of a large number of successful men in their fifties who become suicidal. Born in Arizona, he was raised in a rural atmosphere and was the oldest in a family of three children. His father was a hard-working, close-mouthed, moralistic Irishman, physically powerful and intimidating. He expected manly performance from all his children, his eldest son especially. Dr. Murphy's mother was the opposite from her husband. Small, delicate, and gentle, she was the stereotype of nineteenth-century femininity. Her warmth and generosity stood in marked contrast to her husband's power and demands, and people in the town would marvel at how well these two opposites complemented each other.

Tragedy came when the boy was twelve. His mother's frailty could not withstand severe pneumonia and she died. The next six years were difficult, and when Dr. Murphy finally reached his eighteenth birthday, he left the unhappy home to pursue his own life. What followed were twelve years of dedicated hardship as, with rigid determination, he put himself through college and medical school.

Having inherited much of his father's physical power, he earned some money during these years as a professional boxer and carried on a wide assortment of odd jobs. He worked intensely and played hard and soon found alcohol and women were quick roads to the relaxation and fun he sorely needed.

Early in medical school he fell in love and married. Within a year, however, his bride was dead of tuberculosis, and his deep depression was intensified by unrelenting guilt feelings that he should have been able to save her.

Time covered the wounds, however, and he went on to complete medical school successfully and open a private practice in Los Angeles. He quickly became known, liked, and respected in his community. His Irish wit and skill at storytelling made him popular in any group, and if he drank a little too much at times or ran around a little too much, these characteristics only added flair to this likeable person. Furthermore, from the beginning he was able to separate his functions as a physician and that of a fun-loving, Irish storyteller.

Two years out of medical school, he married again. This marriage lasted eighteen years and produced four children. The distress of the earlier years apparently was overcome, and the decades of his thirties and forties were productive, secure, and enjoyable.

Early in his fifties, however, trouble in the form of a quiet, pervasive depression began to form. Drinking increased, he was quarrelsome at home, and he began having serious misgivings about his professional competency—his ability to be the kind of doctor he felt he had to be. He would express, from time to time, that his life was becoming meaningless, that his children did not really respect him but only the money that he was able to supply them.

Everyone was demanding from him, and no one was concerned about him, he felt. "Why do I have to be a doctor," he once said in the midst of depression. "I don't want to be a doctor. Why do I have to look after other people and hear their problems all the time?"

His discontent took the form of increased sexual activity, which, when his wife discovered it, resulted in cross and angry words and in her moving out and impulsively filing for divorce. With this breakup of his home, his drinking increased even more. His depression became deeper, and he began to age markedly. He impulsively married again and lived a very unhappy and tormented nine months until this wife, too, finally was goaded into leaving. Then there came a plateau in his feelings when he began to settle down and once again turn seriously to his practice of medicine. In another six months he was married again to a depressed, sickly woman, who was plagued with migraine headaches and who seemed to need him. It was about at this time that he was introduced to a local Baptist church, and for the first time in his life, began to show religious interest. He not only would attend church every Sunday but became very active in the boards and committees of the church, contributing generously both in money and in time. In addition, he would have long talks with the pastor, a young man recently out of seminary who was filled with energy and creative ideas. About three months after beginning to attend the church, he made a fundamental decision and "gave his life to Christ." He continued in active participation in the life of the congregation and made significant contributions to the new church building they were erecting. The long conversations with the pastor continued as he tried to work out his feelings of depression, guilt, anxiety, and the pervading sense of meaninglessness. For awhile his drinking fell off, but it slowly began to resume.

He had three car accidents within three months. He escaped from the first accident without any physical injury, but the car was almost totally destroyed. In the second accident he suffered a broken nose, which he doctored himself. The third accident took place on a dark night when he was drunk and, missing a turn, slammed into a telephone pole. He was unhurt, but a neighbor notified the police, and shortly thereafter he was presented with a summons to appear for trial on the charge of drunk driving.

Three months prior to his death, Dr. Murphy, who was still seeing his pastor on a regular basis, was becoming increasingly agitated, suffering more intensity in his feelings of guilt, incompetency, and insecurity; and he began talking about suicide. The subject came up in the pastoral counseling interviews with more and more frequency but without resolution. He would continually ask himself the question, What is there to live for? and he was unable to find any answers. His pastor encouraged him to become more active in his profession, to enlarge his practice, to rejoin the medical school faculty and take up teaching again, but Dr. Murphy would reply that he had not the energy to do these things. The pastor took no other action.

On the Saturday of his death, the doctor had three telephone conversations during the afternoon. At two o'clock he called his wife and said that he would be home late, that he was especially busy at the office that day. At 3:00 P.M. his wife called him to see how he was coming along, and he seemed to be in good spirits, saying that he was finishing earlier than he had anticipated and would be home in time to take her to dinner. The final call was made at 3:30 P.M. when Dr. Murphy called his pastor with whom he had a counseling appointment on Sunday afternoon. He called to cancel. The pastor accepted the cancellation without inquiry and inquired if Dr. Murphy would be in church the next morning. The doctor replied, "I'll be there (pause) if I'm able." The pastor responded to this by trying to humor him out of his depression. He said that Dr. Murphy had "better be there"—that he had written a sermon "directly for him, and he was going to give it to him right between the eyes." The humor fell flat and the doctor simply hung up. The pastor, feeling embarrassed, let it go.

When Dr. Murphy did not return home that night for

dinner with his wife, she was annoyed and disappointed, but didn't take it too seriously. Frequently he would be called to the hospital to sit with a critically ill patient, or simply go out drinking and poker playing with the boys, and often he would forget to let her know. She had a TV dinner and retired early.

Something stirred in her the next morning, however, as she awoke in the sunlit room and reached her hand over to find the space next to her in bed empty. She became frightened and concerned and called a friend who lived near the doctor's office to investigate for her. He discovered the physician lying on his treatment table, dead of the overdose of barbiturates.

MRS. LLOYD

Women, in the same age group, can also represent a high suicidal risk. Mrs. Lloyd is characteristic of this group in many ways. "To know Mrs. Lloyd is to like her." That's what everyone said. That's what they said in the church that she had attended for so many years, the church where she sang in the choir and worked in the women's group and helped the youth program; and that's what they said in the hairdressing shop where she worked part time—that to know Mrs. Lloyd is to like her. Full of energy, cheerful, happy, incessantly chattering about various topics of the day, this fifty-five-year-old woman was well known in her small, suburban town, having lived there for most of her adult life and having raised her two children, her seventeen-year-old daughter and her twenty-one-year-old son, presently fighting in Viet Nam. Her husband, working in the construction business, was a quiet sort of man, whom people did not know as well. But he was a likable sort, and the family was as normal as any on the street.

Mrs. Lloyd was raised in a small town in Missouri, and had moved to California while she was still in her teens. She responded enthusiastically to California's emotional climate and the people she met here, as did her entire family. Her two brothers, both older than she, soon married and moved away. She met her husband while she was attending junior college, and they were married shortly thereafter. Dropping college at this point, she attended hairdressing school so that she could add to the family income. Four years later she became pregnant and gave birth to her son, and then in another four years, her daughter came.

There was little to distinguish this family from any other family in town. They were accepted, well liked, and fit into the community. Their social life was moderately active with the main sources of entertainment being beer for Mr. Lloyd and television for them both. They would have fights from time to time, but for the most part her husband would withdraw from any overt disagreement with her. Things ran pretty much the way she decided, and when Mr. Lloyd got bored at home there was always the friendly group in the local tavern that he enjoyed.

When she was fifty-one she became aware of certain physical symptoms that caused her concern. She went to her family physician, and after a series of tests which revealed some malignant growths, it was decided that she needed major surgery which included a radical mastectomy and a full hysterectomy. She went through this ordeal with no signs whatsoever of depression or upset. She was always completely optimistic, saying that her Christian faith would buoy her up under any circumstances. She and her husband never discussed the operations or what would happen if they were not successful. Her doctor was amazed, describing her as being always cheerful and in good spirits, as if nothing were bothering her. She never complained, never asked for anything, and was always happy.

She came through the operation successfully, and soon after was able to regain her normal active life. She was now working full-time at the hairdressing shop and was still carrying a full load of church responsibilities. It was only in the evening after supper, when her husband would be out bowling or shooting pool with the boys (he was doing more of that these days than ever before) that things would change. The drinking that used to stop with a cocktail before dinner now continued after dinner. At first, a few times a week, and now almost every night, she was crying herself to sleep. Sometimes she would talk to her daughter, giving hints that she felt herself more and more left out of the family arrangements and considerations— that she was feeling that no one needed her. Back in the old days, she would say, when the children were small, they would make many demands on her and she would enjoy filling them; but now with her son in Viet Nam, her daughter very active in her own high school life, and her husband home less, she began to feel that the family was dissolving around her and that there was no longer any place for her.

Her daughter Mary became aware of the increasing depression and attempted to talk to her father about it, but he refused to take the situation seriously, accusing Mary of being melodramatic and reading into the situation trouble which was not there. Left on her own, then, Mary did what she thought best and tried to be especially helpful to her mother, doing much of the cleaning and gradually taking over preparation of meals when her mother had been drinking too much to do that comfortably. Mary's intention was to show concern and helpfulness; the effect was that the mother felt less and less needed and more and more outside the family. Out of her concern and her anxiety Mary began to berate her mother for her heavy drinking, and Mrs. Lloyd would retort in anger that Mary had no right to judge her and that she might not see her like this very many times more. Mary felt the burden of responsibility keenly and at the same time was confused. Her father had told her that she was misperceiving the seriousness of the situation, and whenever she was with her mother outside of the house, she would observe that her mother was her old self—happy, cheerful, outgoing, with no signs of the depression that was so evident at home.

About six weeks before Christmas on a Tuesday afternoon, Mrs. Lloyd returned from her job at the hairdressers about three o'clock in the afternoon. She went to visit a neighbor who had been ill and stayed until about six. She appeared to be in high and gay spirits, when she returned. It was clear to Mary that her mother had been drinking. No one else was home. Mr. Lloyd and his son, recently returned from Viet Nam, were out barhopping. The mother and daughter got into an argument over the mother's drinking, and Mary became upset, frustrated, and hurt and left to go for a walk in the park.

She was gone about an hour, and when she came back about seven o'clock the house was quiet. Glancing into her mother's bedroom and seeing her already in bed, Mary fixed her own supper and watched television until about ten-thirty when her father and brother returned. Then she went to bed. The men had one more drink and then each retired. The next morning Mrs. Lloyd was found dead with an empty sleeping-pill bottle on her bedstand, a suicide.

JOHNNY

Johnny had never been very communicative with his parents, but then that really wasn't very unusual in a seventeen-year-old high school junior, especially one who had as many interests as he did. His parents looked upon him as being a normal boy, and although they were aware of some occasional depressions, they were not overly concerned about them. They usually had a realistic cause, like a fight with his girlfriend, and they never lasted for more than a day or two. The other facts of Johnny's life seemed to outweigh any suspicion they might have had that Johnny was soon to die by suicide.

He had always been a fairly good student, but lately things were going even better than normal. His last report card had been all *A*'s and *B*'s and the family was very proud of this. Johnny, himself, seemed to have good feelings of satisfaction over this accomplishment. The family was stable —his father owned and operated a successful service station in the area, and his mother was a pleasant, concerned woman, who was a housewife. He had one older brother, Hank, with whom he had the normal conflicts and fights. Hank was several years older than Johnny, and the two had grown apart when Hank was drafted for two years in the service. He was back now and fully employed by an aircraft company. Although Hank continued to live in his parents' home, he and Johnny lived separate lives.

The family had moved into the pleasant, lower middle-class area six years before. Johnny had seemed to fit into his peer culture there. He had a full term in Little League, at which he enjoyed moderate success, and was generally considered by those around him to be a member of the group. The only discipline problem of any significance took place when he was in junior high school. A student had handed him a marijuana cigarette through the fence to deliver to another boy, and this transaction was observed by a teacher who immediately apprehended Johnny and took him to the police station. The parents were notified and the school, trying to keep a hard line on drug traffic, had him expelled. Johnny's family was angry about this because they felt that the school was overreacting, and they placed Johnny in another junior high school nearby. The incident was soon forgotten, and there was no evidence that Johnny had any other contact with drugs, although drugs were common in his age group in this area.

Johnny adjusted well to high school. Although his interest in sports fell off slightly, he developed a new interest, common to boys of that age—cars. He joined an automobile club which was sponsored by one of the school counselors and became very active in it. He had definite skill in building and rebuilding motors and enjoyed racing on the weekends on the track provided by the community. On weekends he would wash the family car and play with it, obviously gaining great satisfaction from this. It wasn't long before he decided that he needed a car of his own, and although he was still too young to have a driver's license, he began working on two jobs, one in a car wash and the other as a stock boy, in order to save money so that he would be able to have a car when he was old enough.

Another discovery that Johnny made upon entry into high school was girls, especially one girl, Susan. Johnny and Susan started going together in their freshman year. She lived near him, and the two hit it off from the beginning. Although Johnny would occasionally date other girls, his clear preference was for Susan. By the time they were sophomores, it was well known that they were going steady.

Things began to go badly for Johnny at the beginning of his junior year. For one thing, he began to have arguments with Susan. Although he was as dedicated to her as ever, Susan was beginning to expand her social activities in ways that did not include Johnny. They would have fights when they did date, and Susan began standing Johnny up when she had better offers. Johnny became frantic at this pattern. He would go into a sudden and deep depressions, weep, and have strong feelings of rage, frustration, and helplessness. His mother, who was somewhat in touch with his experiences, would respond by telling him that it really would be better for him to date other girls. He would respond that this was impossible, that he didn't want to date other girls, he only wanted Susan. In spite of all his efforts, the relationship continued to deteriorate, and he saw Susan less and less as she continued to break dates with him and became outspoken in an obvious effort to break the relationship entirely. Johnny responded to this by becoming more depressed and losing interest in his other activities.

The second area of stress for Johhny came early in October when he was injured in football practice. A sharp tackle from one of his teammates in a scrimmage game pulled some ligaments in his leg. This was very painful and meant that Johnny would be sidelined for a number of weeks, possibly for the whole season. This was the second time that he had been injured this fall.

Soon after this, Johnny decided that the car club, which had taken so much of his time in the last couple of years, no longer commanded any interest. He became angry with the way that it was being run and abruptly resigned. The interpretation that his parents made of this action was that he was beginning to grow up and his interest would soon shift to other more mature things. But there was not to be time for this to happen. About three weeks later on a Saturday, Johnny came home from work in high spirits because he had just been paid and he had a date with Susan for that night. He returned ten dollars that he had borrowed from his mother and took a shower. Grabbing a quick supper, he hurried to Susan's house, only to find that she had stood him up again and had gone out with someone else. Johnny became depressed. Leaving Susan's house, he went over to his friend Jeff's home and there met another friend of Jeff's. The three boys went cruising around the city area and obtained some pills. At about eleven o'clock, at a local hamburger stand, Johnny, now in the possession of about sixty pills, commented to his friends that he was going home and kill himself. The friends, who had heard similar threats from Johnny in the preceding weeks, did not take him seriously and ignored the statement. A few minutes later Johnny showed them his pills and asked if they thought this would be enough to kill him. Again, they did not take it seriously and said, sure, they thought that it would be. Johnny left them about eleven-thirty that evening.

He was home about midnight and called Susan. She

answered the phone and thought that Johnny sounded drunk. Johnny told her that if she wasn't going to be his girl anymore he was going to kill himself. Susan became angry at what seemed to her to be an attempt at manipulation and told Johnny that he simply had to realize that she was interested in other things now and hung up on him.

At about 1:00 A.M. Johnny's mother awakened, hearing Johnny vomiting in the bathroom. She arose and went in, and Johnny told her that everything was going to be all right now, not to worry. About 2:00 A.M. his brother came home and fell into the other twin bed in the room that they shared, noticing nothing unusual. It was the next morning about ten o'clock, after Johnny did not come to breakfast, that they found him dead. The autopsy revealed a massive overdose of barbiturates.

Personality Dynamics

Although the dynamics of suicide are unique to each case, there are some common emotional characteristics that we can observe in these three cases. When such people as Dr. Murphy, Mrs. Lloyd, and Johnny become suicidal, two basic conditions are usually present. Strong increasing *stress* combines with a diminishing ability to cope with even normal problems. The trapped, hopeless, and helpless feelings that are produced by this kind of situation are experienced as being both intolerable and inescapable, and the victim feels as though suicide is the only way out, the only solution.

Stress must be measured in terms of how it is experienced by the person himself. In the case of Dr. Murphy, for example, the summons to appear in court on the drunk driving charge would normally constitute a stress which could easily be taken in stride. In this case, however, it represented an intolerable exposure and curtailment of freedom that he could not accept. Coming as it did on the top of other significant stresses, the divorce from an important eighteen-year marriage, two subsequent marital failures, increased drinking, and troubles with his medical practice, it provided the final difficulty that he was unable to tolerate.

In the case of Mrs. Lloyd, the argument with her daughter on the night of her death was a final rejection that mobilized all the long, repressed grief and depression from her serious operation several years prior. This, coupled with the subsequent inattention of her husband, was more than she could handle.

Adolescent boys break up with girls everyday, but the stress coming at this time for Johnny presented him with such intense feelings of rejection that he could not, on this night, find within himself the strength to go on.

As we shall see in subsequent case illustrations, the stresses for men that are often mentioned in suicide notes and recur routinely in suicide case studies include retirement, widowerhood, failing physical powers, and failures in business. For women the common stresses that end in suicides are troubles within the home, especially being or feeling abandoned by the important man, or men in her life and made to feel unappealing in a total kind of way. Other important stresses among suicidal women include other direct attacks on her femininity, such as the experience of hysterectomy and mastectomy or, in some cases, the simple process of aging, which can be devastating to a woman who has invested her sense of self-esteem in her youthfulness and physical attractiveness. For adolescents the stress of being unable to fulfill parental expectations, the feeling of rejection which hits at the heart of one's sexual identity, and sometimes the stress of shame and guilt at homosexual or sadistic thinking can result in suicide.

Feelings of being unwanted and unneeded affect all age and population groups, and if these feelings coming from significant other people are strong enough and global enough, they can present sufficient stress to result in suicidal death.

The *ability to cope* with stress is a more difficult quality to measure or to describe. When feelings of self-esteem are high, when there have been enough positive interpersonal experiences in one's past that he feels worthwhile as a person, he will normally be able to deal with most stress in an appropriate and competent way and not feel that his basic worth as a human being is in jeopardy. When one has not had the benefit of these early feeding and caring experiences, however, or, for some reason, has been unable to incorporate them and build on them, he will be left with grave uncertainty about his own self-worth and will be more likely to collapse under the force of continued severe stress not having the personality reserves to bring into the struggle. When this happens, he may be overwhelmed and become suicidal.

Erik Erikson talks about this quality of self-esteem as coming from infancy, and he refers to it as being a "basic trust in life." Most suicidal people have strong feelings of alienation and isolation, and these often seem to develop early in life if he has suffered what Erikson calls "bad mothering." If he has been the victim of a broken home, either from death or divorce, and especially if he had to tolerate the suicide of a parent, this failure of basic trust can be acute.

Another major characteristic of the ability to cope has to do with the individual's ability to recognize when he needs outside help, his ability to mobilize that help, and his willingness to accept that help. Even persons of relatively weak ego structure often avoid serious suicidal crises if they are able to accept the limitations of their own ego strength and are able to devise ways of supplementing this with the helpfulness of other people. Countless suicides have been avoided by the timely assistance of significant other people who have made available to the suffering victim their own personal warmth and strength in a supportive and helpful way.

There are a significant number of people, however, who, having limited ego strength, at the same time resent, reject, and refuse help from other people. Sometimes this refusal is rationalized by the suicidal person as being a matter of pride. Dr. Murphy, for example, throughout his adult life had seen himself as being a person upon whom other people would lean and he could not bring himself to solicit the kind of help that might have saved his life. Another example of this is Mrs. Lloyd, who, although going through a serious, depressing operation and subsequent marital difficulty was never able to let down her front of cheerfulness and optimism and permit the feelings of grief and dependency to become apparent so that her physician, friends, husband, and clergyman could respond to her need and help her. She interpreted her husband's waning interest in the years subsequent to the operation as being a commentary on her scarred body. It might be equally true that he was responding to her facade of self-sufficiency which he experienced as rejection in the sense of not being needed. In some people the refusal to accept help has other dynamics. Some dependent people are so angry at their own sense of dependency and so envious at another's sense of sufficiency that they have a strong need to render the helper impotent, and they do this by refusing to let him help. Some people are so dedicated to this neurosis that they die in preservation of it.

Whatever the personality dynamics involved, the inability to request or accept help when it is needed is a common characteristic of seriously suicidal people.

The Build-up to Suicide

Another characteristic of suicidal behavior that we see exemplified in these cases is that suicidal behavior always has a history behind it. Although in some cases it may appear to break upon the scene suddenly and without warning, the fact is that the drive toward suicide has been building up slowly often for a matter of years prior to the first attempt.

When people begin to feel the effects of the stress and begin to falter in their ability to handle it in creative ways, they usually will search for alternative methods of escaping from the bad feelings. Most suicidal people have a recent history of an increase in drinking as in the case of both Dr. Murphy and Mrs. Lloyd, while others have a pattern of increased pill-taking to help them sleep at night or feel better during the day. Still others who think that their bad feelings are caused by other people, will break off old relationships, old styles of living, or perhaps take on new relationships, such as a sexual affair, in the effort to do away with the feelings of loneliness, irritation, failure, guilt, or abandonment. When these alternative ways of dealing with the bad feelings fail, the buildup toward suicide is accelerated. The person will then begin thinking about suicide, feeling that his situation is not capable of resolution. The next step in the buildup is pondering alternate ways of committing suicide. The normal suicidal individual will think of several different alternatives and will consider these for some time, finally making a selection. The development of the suicidal plan is a critical stage in the buildup toward death and may open the door to a suicide rehearsal or suicide attempt.

This buildup to suicide may take months or years. It serves two functions: to make the victim more comfortable with the thought of killing himself and to provide a warning for those who care about him.

Communication

The myth that those who talk about suicide seldom do it, has been proved both erroneous and dangerous. Suicidal communications are an integral part of the build-up toward suicide and should be taken very seriously.

As mentioned above, many people have extreme difficulty in asking for help. Sometimes from feelings of pride, fear of rejection, anger, or shame, people frequently find it necessary to disguise the fact that they need help and that they need help from specific people. Instead of asking directly, they will engage in both verbal and behavioral hints aimed, often unconsciously, at informing people near them that they are in emotional trouble. Statements like,

"You won't have to worry about me after next Tuesday," or, "You and the family will be better off without me," are often disguised invitations for the listener to take the initiative into further inquiry into what the victim is feeling and planning. Actions such as making a will or selecting a cemetery plot can often be a clue that the person is planning his own demise. Putting things in order, resigning from church boards and committees, as if one were tidying up to go on a long trip are often telltale signs. Almost all suicidal people attempt to communicate with significant other people in their own lives prior to killing themselves. This communicating behavior, sometimes taking the form of a suicide attempt, has been called, the cry for help, by Shneidman and Farberow. It is as if the person is desperately trying by indirection to do what he cannot do by direct means—to get the attention of someone close to him and elicit a warm response from him.

The problem is that these clues are often not heard at all, or they are misinterpreted. The response that comes back to the suicidal victim is frequently one of anger, rejection, or apathy. This confirms his neurotic hypothesis that there is no help avialable, no one cares, and that he might just as well die.

Ambivalence

Another important characteristic of suicidal people is the concept of ambivalence. Ambivalence is the coexistence of contradictory attitudes and desires at the same time. In answer to the question, "Did Dr. Murphy, Mrs. Lloyd, and Johnny really want to die?" the answer must take seriously both sides of their personality conflict. On the one hand, the clear fact is that they are dead—that they did want to die. On the other hand, it can be said with equal accuracy that all of them wanted to live. Both answers are true.

Johnny, for example, made overt communications to several people—his friends at the hamburger stand and his girl over the telephone—telling them what he was about to do and, in effect, asking to be prevented from doing it. The fact that none of his friends responded in a helpful way is a good example of how even direct suicidal communications can be overlooked and not taken seriously. It is also an example of a basic ambivalence in Johnny of wanting to be rescued and prevented from killing himself. Mrs. Lloyd took the overdose of pills when she knew that her daughter would be returning to the home shortly and the chances of her husband coming home soon were very good. Any direct inquiry as to how she was feeling that night, any attempt to arouse her, would have resulted in her rescue, and the life side of her ambivalence would have prevailed. Dr. Murphy made several communications on the day of his death, even phoning his pastor and cancelling an appointment and giving an equivocal answer to whether he would be in church the next day. There was a side to him that wanted to live and to work out his problems even though they seemed to be, at that moment, insoluble. This basic conflict, called ambivalence, present in all suicidal persons, is the explanation of why so many people make suicide attempts in the presence of other people. They are hoping to be stopped and rescued, even as they are wanting to die.

Crisis

Most people who are suicidal are intensely suicidal only for a short period of time, and this is usually in reaction to a specific newly introduced stress or rejection. The suicidal crisis may last only for a few hours, and if the victim can survive during this period of time he may never be suicidal again.

If Johnny had been prevented from killing himself on that night the chances are very strong that he would not have made any more suicide attempts, and the same would be true of Mrs. Lloyd and Dr. Murphy. Most people who are suicidal are intensely so for only a brief period of time —a matter of hours or days—and if suicide prevention can be effective during this limited period the life-preserving side of the ambivalence will return to dominance, and if the person is receiving help, the danger of suicide will fall off dramatically, at least until the introduction of a whole new pattern of stress. All these concepts have direct application to the process of suicide prevention, which is the topic of the next chapter.

Depression

No chapter on the dynamics of suicide would be complete without a discussion of depression. Although not all depressed people are suicidal and not all suicides are depressed, yet depression is a common factor in many suicides. The feelings of depression include feelings of low self-esteem, feelings of incompetence and failure. The depressed person often experiences loss of appetite, the inability to sleep or the inability to awaken, as well as a loss of sexual interest and capability. His thinking processes may be slowed down, and he may move slower and feel heavy and despondent.

The depressed person will view his situation as unsatisfying and flat, and see no way in which it will ever improve. He feels trapped in his feelings of hopelessness and helplessness. The depression can also seriously affect an individual's ability to perceive. He is not as alert to possibilities and often grossly distorts communications that are coming to him. He will often experience humor as being hostile, helpfulness as being rejection, and he'll feel distant and separated from any feelings of joy or satisfaction. Often he is literally incapable of entertaining alternative courses of action. His problem-solving abilities may be negligible, and often he will feel as if he were in a deep pit from which there is no exit. Unable to perceive alternatives or create alternatives, he assumes there are no alternatives, and thus his depression becomes cyclical and intensifies itself.

Frequently, a depressed person will not even know he is depressed. He will simply know that things are not right and that something is seriously wrong. Instead of identifying that he is feeling like a bad person, he will think that he is a bad person; being unable to distinguish the depressed feelings of being bad from some actual state of badness.

The meaning of a depression is usually that the individual is not being taken care of. He is being cut off from the warmth of human concern and of being cared for. He is lonely and abandoned, sometimes emotionally and sometimes physically, and he needs help.

Special Situations

The case studies so far have portrayed relatively normal people who are to be found in almost any community in America. Dr. Murphy, Mrs. Lloyd, and Johnny might be members of any church congregation, and in fact their suicides were a surprise to those who knew them. But there are high suicide rates for certain other groups who are not comfortably integrated into the major culture.

Anita and June are both young girls, who, because of certain personality characteristics, may never feel at home in their society, and are suicidal. Mr. Harris, too, has trouble maintaining supportive relationships.

ANITA

Anita is an attractive, bright, twenty-one-year-old girl, who lists her occupation as actress, model, and dancer. She called the Suicide Prevention Center after making a suicide attempt, as she put it, by "cutting my wrists, turning on the gas, and then swallowing poison." The result of this grand gesture was that she vomited the pills, turned off the gas, and had her wrists repaired by a physician. When asked why she did all this, she replied that she did not really know; that she was just tired of fighting and living, but that now she wanted help.

Anita is a prototypic example of a certain kind of girl that is often seen at the Suicide Prevention Center in Los Angeles. Usually only in their twenties or thirties, they already have a history of suicide attempts as one expression of their characteristics of self-abuse and self-punishment.

So intensive and self-feeding is their predeliction to suffering and so intrinsic to their character, that even the term "masochist" seems too weak to accurately describe their life-style. Dr. Robert E. Litman, chief psychiatrist at the Los Angeles center, coined the term, "malignant masochist," to portray more accurately the self-perpetuating nature of the masochism that pervades their entire personalities.

Like most malignant masochists, Anita reports an unpleasant childhood. She describes her mother as being a very sick, masochistic person herself, who kept the household in constant uproar. When Anita was eight years old, her mother abruptly told her that she was an illegitimate child of an unknown father. Anita recalls her feelings of bewilderment, confusion, and resentment. She reports also that she never got along well with her stepfather and that they had an open break after he tried to molest her sexually when she was ten or eleven. When she reported the incident to her mother she was blamed for provoking it.

Anita left home as quickly as she could by getting married at eighteen to a European engineer. She was a good wife because she did the things that good wives do: She had sex only with her husband and stayed home keeping a clean house for him. Anita's marriage broke up when she left her husband because he "made her" have an abortion that she did not want. She did not think the issue worth fighting about. Her departure was abrupt, and she has never seen him again.

Anita then drifted into show business, becoming a dancer. She had a quick succession of boyfriends, and it was the breakup with one of these that led to her most recent suicide attempt. She had gone to Las Vegas with her boyfriend and with the prospect of a job as a dancer in one of the major hotels. When she found that the job did not pay what she had been promised, she felt rejected and turned to her boyfriend for support. He, however, had become preoccupied with some of the other attractions in Las Vegas and treated her coldly. She was upset by this and tried to threaten him by saying that she would return to Hollywood and become a prostitute. When her boyfriend retorted that this might be a good plan. Anita responded with a severe and chaotic depression, making the triple suicide attempt. She was rescued only by the providential intervention of her theatrical agent.

Anita is a severely disturbed girl, characterized by schizophrenic confusion and hysterical defenses against feelings. She reacts to her pervasive feelings of internal rottenness in a variety of ways, including multiple suicide attempts. But suicide is only one expression of the malignant masochism.

She easily becomes upset when people fight or argue in her presence, and she experiences periodic detachment, chronic daydreaming, withdrawal, compulsive and circular thinking which frequently reaches the point where she is no longer in control. "Sometimes," she said, "it is hard for me to establish contact. Sometimes I think I want to stay in a haze." She frequently feels confused about her own feelings and, as she puts it, "often feels confused about what it is she feels confused about."

Psychological test results confirm Anita's description of herself as being a hypermanic person who experiences overwhelming feelings of confusion, looseness, and disorganization of thought, and who is easily overwhelmed by her own anxiety.

Anita has deep uncertainty about her own feminine identity. She likes to evaluate herself as being successful as a woman on the basis that she looks like a woman, and that she is able to perform in the way women are suppose to perform. She took some pride in being a good wife because she was able to do the things that society sees good wives doing. Furthermore, she tends to drift to those occupations which are clearly identifiable from a cultural viewpoint as being feminine occupations such as modeling, dancing, and being a cocktail waitress. But beneath this feminine facade, there is a deep insecurity and uncertainty about what it means to feel feminine or to be a woman.

Instead of experiencing the good, beautiful, and affirmative feelings of womanhood, Anita experiences herself as being basically bad, rotten, and disgusting. It is against this fundamental self-identification that she fights her desperate, defensive battles. But in spite of her strongest attempts, her basic negative self-concept makes it all but impossible for her to have any but painful and destructive relationships. It is this self-image of rottenness that lies behind her thoughts of suicide.

Anita usually lives with thoughts of suicide, and suicide attempts have become a characteristic way of handling stress. She offers the hypothesis that she makes suicide attempts the way other people get drunk or have fights. It is a way for her to release emotional tension, or, to use her words, it is an emotional way out. The attempts are usually made by ingesting pills and cutting. The pills provide opportunity for erotic sensations and fantasy as she begins to lose consciousness. Cutting, too, gives some sensual pleasure, and at the same time releases built-up, internal tension.

Anita's history includes multiple suicide attempts beginning in childhood. She made her first attempt at the age of fourteen when she took an overdose of pills and cut herself. Some of her attempts were highly lethal, as the one a year ago when she took 120 sleeping pills and tranquilizers. Although she had made some tentative provision for rescue, she was comatose for three days after having her stomach pumped and almost died. Her last two attempts, she reports, were honest attempts to die, although even in these she was aware of ambivalence when she reached the point that she thought she was actually dying. The other attempts, she now feels, were attempts to find some sensual pleasure or to avoid the pain of built-up emotional pressure.

Anita will seek help in time of crisis, but once the immediate stress has been resolved she feels no motivation for continuing therapy. She moves on in hysterical optimism that things will be better next time, and usually there is another man such as Tony to capture her interest.

Tony is a "beautiful man" who drives a big Cadillac, carries a gun, associates routinely with criminals, and treats Anita cruelly. Anita half realizes that Tony is bad for her, that the relationship is doomed to suffering with an unpleasant termination. But in spite of this half-awareness, she continues to pursue the relationship because she thinks she loves him.

The prognosis for Anita is that she probably will not kill herself, at least in the foreseeable future. Instead, she will continue in her own severely disturbed, masochistic style of life, suffering confusion and bewilderment as to why things happen to her. She will make more suicide attempts, and they are likely to increase in seriousness. She will continue to find confirmation for her feelings of rottenness.

JUNE

Another example of a severely disturbed person who is chronically actively suicidal is June, a twenty-three-year-old single girl who could be termed a "harlequin."

The concept of the Harlequin has a long and interesting history in mythology and literature which has been ably traced by David C. McClelland in an article, "The Harlequin Complex." [1] Briefly, Harlequin is a charming clown who dresses in a multicolored, diamond-patterned suit and a black mask. He is noted for his acrobatic tricks and practical jokes, which he performs with the aid of his magic bat or slapstick. His seductive charm is directed toward young and innocent girls, whom he seeks to capture with promises of exquisite erotic pleasure. He comes mysteriously and sometimes invisibly in the night and is usually associated with illicit, forbidden love.

The true goal of the Harlequin's approach, however, is death. In some of the mythological stories, as traced by McClelland, the Harlequin appears as death himself, a charming, and yet invisible and eerie, visitor. In other accounts he is the agent of death, whose task it is to deliver the young girls into his master's dark realm. As the girl gives herself over to the charm and seduction of the Harlequin she is, in fact, giving herself over to death and placing herself in his control to be transported over the river Styx. The idea of death as a lover in mythology is not, of course, exclusive with the Harlequin. But the Harlequin does provide a convenient symbol for a certain group of malignant masochists.

In addition to experiencing all the characteristics of malignant masochists like Anita—the predeliction to suffering, confusion, preoccupation with suicide, and internal feelings of rottenness—this group, whom we call harlequins,

[1] David C. McClelland, in *The Study of Lives*, ed. Robert W. White (New York: Atherton Press, 1963).

53

personifies and eroticizes the concept of death to the point where they respond in an excited, positive, and passionate manner. In their fantasies and dreams they picture death as a warm, concerned being who offers them cessation from the pain of life and the commencement of pleasure in death.

June has a long and involved history with drugs, prostitution, devious sexual behavior, suicide attempts, and other disturbances.

When asked what death means to her, her answer was:

"Death to me is beautiful—beautiful and peaceful. I write poetry, I write poems, death is my lover. . . . Not too long ago I was sitting in the waiting room, and I just felt death standing next to me with his hand on my shoulder comforting me.

"I had a vision or something, I don't know, hallucination or something. It was a long thing but it culminated: I was walking down this corridor—I was just walking, this warm light came down like this on either side of me, and this hand came down, not down to me, but just down, and this voice said to me, 'You can come home now, you've suffered enough.' I wasn't afraid, I didn't feel—I didn't feel—I really felt that's what was happening. I have this thing about death standing next to me with his hand on me, comforting. He is a man in a robe, a dark robe. He has no face, but he has a very gentle hand, and he has wings like . . . I have heard the flapping.

"I mean it, I'm not just being poetic or anything. It's somebody very comforting. It's like my lover. I'm having a love affair with death.

"If they took death away from me and didn't give me

anything to hang on to. . . . This is what I felt—like death cares for me."

When June makes her suicide attempts, she takes great care to make herself beautiful. She said at one time that she never would commit suicide by shooting herself because this would disfigure her body and spoil her presentation to death, her lover.

MR. HARRIS

Another group of cases which represent extremely high suicide risk is represented by Mr. Harris a lonely sixty-four-year-old man, one of thousands who inhabit the downtown sections of large metropolitan areas. Very little is known about the background and the personality structure of these men because they usually live lonely, isolated lives with only the most superficial contact with other people. Most have lost touch with their own history and tradition, and as a result, they are very difficult to research.

Mr. Harris was walking through an amusement park in Los Angeles one day in late spring and paused at a shooting gallery which was, at the time very busy. He waited in line patiently until it was his turn. He paid the quarter, received the loaded pistol, and then, in front of witnesses, carefully cocked the gun, turned the pistol toward himself, and fired. He died an hour later in an emergency hospital. The autopsy revealed that there was neither alcohol nor barbiturates in the blood and that he had not eaten in some time.

The investigation that the police and the coroner's office made subsequent to his death revealed only that Mr. Harris lived in a residence hotel and had lived there for a little over a year. During that time he had made no close friends and had no intimate associations; no one knew anything about his history or any family. He was unemployed. People in the hotel stated that he was a pleasant man who never caused any trouble and lived his patient, isolated, lonely life, dying when his financial resources were depleted.

Conclusion

Suicide is not a function of social class and transcends most psychiatric categories. Dr. Murphy and Mr. Harris have little in common except for the fact that they both ended life by suicide. June and Mrs. Lloyd would not want to be identified with each other in life, yet they both sought release and relief in death.

The prevention of suicide, however, depends on the ability to identify the main emotional issues and to predict accurately which people are likely to die by their own hands. Such prediction depends on being able accurately to recognize and evaluate the developing suicidal crisis in all kinds of people.

Chapter 2
The Science of Suicidology

"Suicidology" is a term developed by Edwin S. Shneidman, cofounder of the Los Angeles Suicide Prevention Center and first chief of the Center for Studies of Suicide Prevention, a division of the National Institute of Mental Health. It refers to the scientific study of the phenomenon of suicide, drawing information from a wide variety of scientific disciplines.

Through the methods of empirical investigation, the disciplines of sociology and psychology seek to provide better understanding of man's occasional attempts to kill himself.

The Contributions of Sociology

Statistical Findings

The sociological interest in suicide began in the nineteenth century and concerned itself primarily with the accumulation of actuarial data and the attempts to find significant correlations between certain variables.[1]

[1] Some of the early studies which are commonly referred to include: Jean Esquiral, *Mental Maladies: A Treatise on Insanity,* tr. E. K. Hunt (Philadelphia: Lea and Blanchard, 1838); Forbes Winslow, *The Anatomy of Suicide* (London: Renshaw, 1840); Lisle, *Du Suicide, Statistique, Med-*

For the most part, the findings of these studies were comparable with one another. Dublin summarizes the major findings, most of which were consistent with contemporary research. Statistically, men are more likely to commit suicide than women, although women are more likely to attempt suicide than are men; Caucasians more than Negroes; city dwellers more than rural populations; single persons more than married; divorced more than single persons; military personnel more than civilians; and those having no children tend to be more prone to suicide than people who have children. Suicides are more apt to occur during times of peace than in times of war. The suicide rate of Protestants is characteristically higher than that of Catholics, and Catholics higher than Jews.[2]

Sociologists continue to collect actuarial data which provide much valuable information about the nature of suicidal behavior.

Table I compares the suicide rates of several nations. Such figures must be taken with some skepticism, however, because nations differ widely in their methods of collecting data. Leonard Gross in an article on Sweden in *Look Magazine* expressed this when he observed, "Sweden's infamous suicide rate suffers from an honest count that doesn't exist where law or religion condemned the act."

---

icine, *Histoire et Legislation* (Paris: J. B. Baillere, 1856); Louis Bertrand, *Traite du Suicide, Considere dans ses Rapports Avec La Philosophie, La Theologie, La Medicine, et La Jurisprudence* (Paris: J. B. Baillere, 1857); H. Morselli, *Suicide, An Essay on Comparative Moral Statistics* (New York: Appleton, 1882); James O'Dea, *Suicide: Studies on Its Philosophy, Causes and Prevention* (New York: G. P. Putnam & Sons, 1882); Alfred Legoyt, *Le Suicide Ancient et Moderne* (Paris: A. Dronin, 1887); Samuel Strahan, *Suicide and Insanity* (London: Sonnenschein and Company, 1893).

[2] Louis Dublin and Bessie Bunzel, *To Be or Not To Be* (New York: Smith and Haas, 1933).

Table I

Suicide Rate (per 100,000 Population) of the United States and Some Other Major Countries

Country	Year	Rate
United States	1966	10.9
South Africa (white population)	1962	16.9
Cuba	1964	11.3
Canada	1966	8.6
Mexico	1966	8.6
Japan	1965	14.7
West Berlin	1964	41.7
Sweden	1966	20.1
Denmark	1965	19.3
Switzerland	1965	18.1
France	1965	15.0
England and Wales	1966	10.4

SOURCE: World Health Organization, *Epidemiological and Vital Statistics Report: Mortality From Suicide,* 9:243.

Table II traces the suicide rate in the United States since the end of World War II. There appears to be no significant trend in the rate of suicidal deaths, although there is a rise in the number of suicides because of the rise in population.

Table II

Suicide Rates (per 100,000 Population) for the United States from 1945-67

Year	Rate	Year	Rate
1945	11.2	1957	9.8
1946	11.5	1958	10.7
1947	11.5	1959	10.6
1948	11.2	1960	10.6

Year	Rate	Year	Rate
1949	11.4	1961	10.4
1950	11.4	1962	10.9
1951	10.4	1963	11.0
1952	10.0	1964	11.0
1953	10.1	1965	11.0
1954	10.1	1966	10.9
1955	10.2	1967	11.0
1956	10.0		

Mean rate   10.7
Median rate 10.9

SOURCE: *Vital Statistics of the United States*, Vol. II. Mortality. Department of HEW, Public Health Service.

It might also be of interest to compare the incidence of suicide with other forms of violent death.

Table III shows the national suicide rate to be more than twice that of homicide and about half the death rate by automobile accident.

Table III

Comparison of Death Rates from Accidents, Suicide, and Homicide in the United States 1953-62 (Rates per 100,000 Population per Year)

Mode of Death	Rate	Percentage of Total Deaths
All accidents	52.3	5.5
Auto accidents alone	22.0	2.33
Suicide	10.9	1.20
Homicide	4.9	.60

SOURCE: *Vital Statistics of the United States*, Vol. II. Mortality. Department of HEW, Public Health Service.

Table IV shows the number of these deaths in Los Angeles County. These figures are probably comparable with those of any major city in the nation.

Table IV

Comparison of Number of Deaths from Suicide, Auto Accidents, Homicides, and Occupational Accidents in Los Angeles County

	1959-60	1960-61
Suicide	973	937
Homicide	282	296
Auto accidents	935	918
Occupational accidents	108	108

SOURCE: *Biennial Report of the Coroner 1959-61*, Los Angeles County.

Table V shows the breakdown of suicide rates into the variables of age and sex. This is one of the most significant and useful of the statistics. One of the major findings this table demonstrates is the consistent fact that men kill themselves at the rate of about double that of women.

Table V

Suicide Rate (per 100,000 population) by Age and Sex for 1967 in the United States

Ages	Male	Female
10-14	.9	.3
15-19	6.9	2.4
20-24	13.9	4.8
25-29	16.6	6.8
30-34	17.0	8.6
35-39	20.9	10.4
40-44	24.2	10.9

Ages	Male	Female
45-49	25.2	11.5
50-54	29.8	12.7
55-59	33.9	12.2
60-64	35.0	10.6
65-69	30.6	10.1
70-74	35.9	8.5
75-79	38.5	7.1
80-84	46.3	5.8
85 +	50.9	5.5
Total rates all ages	15.5	6.1
Total population both sexes	10.7	

SOURCE: *Vital Statistics of the United States,* Vol. II. Mortality. Department of HEW, Public Health Service.

What the table does not indicate, however, is that the suicide-attempt rate for women is about double that of men. Men characteristically employ more deadly means than women and appear to be less equivocal about wanting to die when they are in a suicidal crisis.

The other major contribution of this table is the pattern of age distribution. Suicide in children under ten is extremely rare and is not significant in terms of any statistical analysis. For men, the suicide rate rises with age, remaining negligible in adolescents, and growing until it presents a major problem in the population group of elderly men.

With women, the pattern is somewhat different. Starting low in adolescence, the rate increases with age, until peaking at the age of fifty, and then falls off somewhat.

Table VI shows the same age groupings, but reports the number of deaths instead of the rates. Men in the fifties report the highest number of suicides, and for women the late forties and early fifties provide the greatest number of suicidal fatalities.

The helping person who is concerned about preventing suicide is, therefore, well advised to be especially concerned about any suicidal communication he receives from a depressed person in any of these dangerous age groups.

Another statistically important characteristic of suicidal persons is their marital status.

Table VI

Number of Suicidal Deaths
in the United States in 1967

Ages	Number of Suicides	
	Male	Female
10-14	94	27
15-19	624	212
20-24	1,047	361
25-29	1,003	411
30-34	927	478
35-39	1,194	613
40-44	1,460	694
45-49	1,448	699
50-54	1,559	706
55-59	1,550	607
60-64	1,328	450
65-69	904	359
70-74	803	249
75-79	611	156
80-84	405	74
85 +	227	40
Totals	15,184	6,136

Total male and female   21,320

Table VII analyzes the 1,171 persons who killed themselves in Los Angeles County in 1968. Especially significant in this table is the rate reported for divorced men (152.0). This is an extremely high figure and must be taken very seriously by any professional who works with men in that population group.

Employment is another factor that many have felt was important in terms of suicidal behavior.

Table VII

Marital Status of Committed
Suicides in Los Angeles County 1968

	Male	Female	Total	Rates (per 100,000)		
				Male	Female	Total
Single	163	55	218	28.8	12.6	21.7
Married	242	188	430	14.5	11.2	12.8
Divorced or separated	215	123	338	152.0	56.7	94.4
Widowed	50	71	121	66.3	21.0	29.3
Don't know	37	27	64	- - - -	- - - -	- - - -
	707	464	1,171			

SOURCE: Department of Statistics, Suicide Prevention Center, Los Angeles.

Table VIII reports the employment status of all those who committed suicide in Los Angeles County in 1968. As the table indicates, most of these were employed in their normal occupation. The one other group that is statistically significant is that of retired men, who comprised a significant number of the suicides of that year.

Table VIII

Employment Status of Committed Suicides in Los Angeles County in 1968 by Percentage

	Male	Female
Employed	75	92*
Unemployed	7	3
Retired	18	5

* Includes being housewife
SOURCE: Department of Statistics, Suicide Prevention Center, Los Angeles.

Another important characteristic of completed suicides is the analysis of the methods that they characteristically employ. For years, death by gunshot wound was, by far, the most common method of committing suicide. As Table IX indicates, barbiturates have taken over as the most common method.

Table IX

Method of Death Employed by Suicide Victims in Los Angeles County 1968 by Sex

Method	Total Number	Male	Female
Gunshot	412	336	76
Barbiturates	458	159	299
Hanging	83	67	16
Carbon Monoxide	85	66	19
Jumping	32	20	12
Plastic bag	17	5	12
Poison	30	17	13
Cutting	19	15	4
Other	35	22	13
	1,171	707	464
Percentage of suicidal deaths	100	60	40

The group of suicides that seems to elicit the most interest from both helping people, and from the population as a whole, is that of the adolescent. In the past few years, there has been much information published misleading some to understand that there is a wave of increased suicide in the United States, and possibly in the rest of the world. A careful study of the available statistics indicates that this is not true—the suicide rate has not risen appreciably among adolescents over the last few decades and we are not experiencing anything unusual in this decade.

Table X charts the major causes of death among the fifteen- to twenty-four-year-old population of the United States in 1964.

Table X

Leading Causes of Death Ages 15-19 and 19-24
in the United States, 1964

Cause of Death	15-19 Years of Age		19-24 Years of Age	
	Rate	Rank	Rate	Rank
Accidents	53.5	1	66.4	1
Malignant neoplasms	7.7	2	9.2	3
Cardiovascular renal disease	5.7	3	10.0	2
Homicide	4.3	4	8.8	4
Suicide	4.0	5	8.4	5

Source: *Vital Statistics of the United States.* Vol. II. Mortality. Department of HEW, Public Health Service.

As the table reflects, death by accident ranks number one as the overwhelming cause of death in this age group. Suicide ranks a poor fifth, with a comparatively low death rate. This is not to imply that the suicide problem among adolescents should be treated lightly, or that suicidal communications by young people should go ignored. Suicide remains, in adolescence as in the older age groups, the number one cause of stigmatizing death, as Shneidman has often pointed out.

The statistics of suicide are indispensable for giving a clear and balanced overview of some of the major characteristics of a problem and of a people who find themselves victims of suicidal impulses. But suicide itself can only be encountered directly, in terms of the single individual who is unhappy and distressed and planning to die. To understand suicide it is necessary to listen to the range and intensity of feelings that lead one to give up on life.

Durkheim

With the publication of Durkheim's major work in 1897, the sociological conception of suicide underwent a major revision. Prior to Durkheim, the actuarial data which had been collected was being interpreted as part of an effort to isolate the conditions under which the individual might be likely to attempt suicide. Durkheim held that the true significance of the statistics is that suicide is primarily a social phenomenon and not an individual one. He defends the thesis that "suicide which appears to be a phenomenon relating to the individual is actually explicable aetiologically with reference to the social structure and its ramifying functions." [3] Society is something more than the sum of its parts. Any society has an existence of its own, and this existence can be studied. This study is the science of sociology.

[3] Emile Durkheim, *Le Suicide: Etude de Sociologie,* tr. Spaulding and Simpson (Glencoe, Ill.: Free Press, 1951), p. 84.

The suicide rate of any society is a product of that society. The fact that Catholics, for example, appear to have a lower suicide rate than Protestants has little to do with the belief-content of their religions or with the attempts they make to discourage suicide by authoritarian prohibition or moral condemnation. The significant difference between them is that the Catholic Church presents a more unified, more closely integrated social community than does Protestantism, and this is the crucial factor.

Similarly, the fact of one's being married per se has little to do with the suicide potential of the person. But marriage is a community, and those who are married and living in a monogamous culture are closer to the social norm and are better integrated into the wider community.

Durkheim held a negative view of the work of the demographers who preceded him. He labeled as "extra social factors" the age, sex, race, heredity of psychopathic states of suicidal persons, and held that they were of little importance. The "cosmic" factors of geography, climate, and religious belief were also incidental. What is determinative is the nature of the society and the individual person's integration into that social framework.

There are three types of suicide, according to Durkheim. The "egoistic" suicide stems from excessive individualism, wherein the person has an inadequate integration within his society. Such a person is not sufficiently dependent on his social group and is left too much to his private interests. His social ties are not meaningful to him, and he does not share the beliefs and practices of a common, intense collective life. People tend to cling longer to an unsatisfactory life if they belong to a group that is meaningful to them, and if they place a higher value on the social bonds than on their own desires and impulses.

"Altruistic" suicide is a reverse phenomenon. When a person is over-integrated into his society and completely subordinates his own desires to the will of the group, he will kill himself if and when his society demands it. We see examples of this in some religious martyrdom, in the *suttee* of the just-widowed Indian woman, and in certain military actions (for example, *hara-kiri*).

The third classification of suicidal behavior which Durkheim identifies is the "anomic." When a person is suddenly confronted by a crisis situation in which there is a "lack of social regulation" or when the "social constraints" are missing, he may not be able to handle suicidal impulses.

In times of catastrophe when the social order is temporarily destroyed, as in the case of some natural disaster, there is no social unity, constraint, or regulation and the suicidal danger rises.

The anomic effect may also be present when the person experiences a sudden increase or decrease of wealth or the loss of a significant other person in his life upon whom he relied for his social definition. Whenever the nature of the person's life is dramatically changed, and his normal social relationships are lost or in a state of chaos, he may be susceptible to anomic suicide.

As we might expect of this early functionalist, Durkheim sees religion as important only insofar as it serves a social purpose. This is evident in his definition of religion: "Religion is in a word the system of symbols by means of which society becomes conscious of itself; it is the characteristic way of thinking of collective existence." [4] Religion is useful

⁴ *Ibid.*, p. 312.

in facilitating social cohesiveness and tends to arise in periods of collective ferment. Insofar as it serves this function, it is an antisuicidal influence. But in modern times, religion has outgrown its usefulness. It no longer claims the respect that it once held and in our time is an anachronism:

> Religion, therefore, modifies the inclination to suicide only to the extent that it prevents man from thinking freely . . . . In a word, we are only preserved from egoistic suicide in so far as we are socialized; but religions can socialize us only in so far as they refuse us the right of free examination. They no longer have, and probably will never again have, enough authority to wring such a sacrifice from us. We therefore cannot count on them to rear barriers to suicide.[5]

Breed

Since Durkheim, sociology has been active in its study of suicide. Warren Breed summarizes contemporary studies of suicide in four categories. The first category has to do with the socio-cultural organization of the society and the extent of integration it displays. This is essentially an elaboration of Durkheim's position.[6]

The second category is the study of the groups and strata within the society and the manner in which they are inter-related in cooperation, competition, and conflict. This emphasis seeks to determine the manner in which the members of the society are attached to these sub-groups. The emphasis here is on demography and actuarial information.

The third area of sociological study considers the nature

---

[5] *Ibid.,* p. 375-76.

[6] Warren Breed, "Suicide and Loss in Social Interaction," in *Essays on Self-Destruction,* ed. Edwin S. Shneidman (New York: Science House, 1967) , p. 188.

of interpersonal social relationships that members of the society experience in their day-to-day experiences with other people. To a large extent, our opinions of ourselves are determined by other peoples' opinions of us, or what we think their opinion of us may be. Much of our social striving is an effort to gain favorable assessment from other people with whom we have contact. When a person is experiencing "downward mobility," when he is "failing" as his society defines "failure," the assessment that he sees in the attitudes of those about him is negative. This negative assessment may be intolerable to him, and a suicidal danger may be present.

Basic to this theory is the concept of "loss" which may refer to the loss of social position and prestige (and the value which society places on it), financial wealth, or the loss (through death or other means) of a loved one. This experience of loss is often found just prior to a suicide attempt.

The fourth area of contemporary study, which Breed defines, is that of the intrapsychic structure and functioning of the individual person and his development from childhood. This is the psychological inquiry, to which we turn in the next section. Dr. Breed points out that all four areas have a contribution to make in a comprehensive understanding of suicidal behavior.

Sociology continues its concern and its investigation of suicide with new and old approaches, but as yet it is not satisfied with its own results. Jack P. Gibbs states: "After more than six decades, we still lack an adequate treatment of suicide as a social and sociological problem." [7]

[7] Jack Gibbs in *Contemporary Social Problems*, ed. R. K. Merton and R. A. Nisbet (New York: Harcourt Brace Jovanovich, 1961).

The Contributions of Psychology

Freud

Dominant among the personality theorists in modern times is Sigmund Freud. Although Freud never wrote a systematic paper on the subject of suicide, the many references throughout his writings indicate that he was well aware of the problem and was concerned about it. Robert E. Litman, M.D., has written one of the most comprehensive accounts of Freud's thinking on suicide.[8]

One of the best-known dynamics of suicide observed by Freud is internalized hostility—the murderous wishes and impulses which are often directed at parents. Seen in terms of the classic oedipal drama, the child experiences great anger and resentment against the like-sexed parent and wishes that he were dead so that the child could replace him in the other's affections. But because these thoughts are magically dangerous, because he fears reprisal for his aggression, and because along with this hate he wants the love of the like-sexed parent also, the murderous wishes are repressed and sometimes turned inward upon the child himself. Freud expressed it in this way: "We have long known it is true that no neurotic harbors thoughts of suicide which he has not turned back upon himself from murderous impulses against others." [9]

A second clinical impression which struck Freud is that guilt is often a result of the oedipal desire, not only in terms of the incest wish, but also concerning the murderous wish. This guilt, and subsequent need for punishment,

---

[8] Litman, in *Essays on Self-Destruction.*
[9] Sigmund Freud, *Standard Edition of Complete Psychological Works* (London: Hogarth Press, 1953-65), Vol. XIV, pp. 247-52.

sometimes takes a suicidal expression. "We find that impulses to suicide in a neurotic turn out regularly to be self-punishment for wishes for someone else's death." [10] The "someone else" may be a sibling as well as a parent.

Another clinical impression which Freud offered is the process of identification with a parent who had died when the child was at an early age.[11] Possibly the parent had suicided, and this appeared to make the suicidal danger especially strong. The desire to join the deceased parent took the patient to suicidal thoughts.

Still another factor was the suicidal person's inability—or unwillingness—to accept the loss of some valued libidinal object. Either from feelings of rage or a sense of abandonment, the loss of the object triggered a suicidal danger as if the person were saying, "I cannot live without you." Freud also noted that revenge was sometimes a strong motivation for self murder, much in the same way as it is in some of the primitive tribes that have been noted earlier. Suicide was also sometimes an escape from humiliation, and at times appeared to be an attempt at communication, what we now know as the cry for help.

As we might expect, Freud was also very much aware of the relationship between death and sexuality, just as he saw the sado-masochistic complex as associated in some cases with suicide.

Yet with all these clinical impressions Freud was unwilling to draw premature theoretical conclusions about the dynamics of suicidal behavior. At a meeting of the Vienna Psychoanalytic Society in 1910, the subject of sui-

[10] *Ibid.*, Vol. X, [1909] pp. 153-318.
[11] This point has been stressed by Gregory Zilboorg in "Suicide among Civilized and Primitive Races," *American Journal of Psychology,* 92 (May 1936) , 1347.

cide was discussed at some length. Although much clinical material was presented, most of it having to do with aggression, Freud refused to draw premature conclusions. He addressed the meeting:

> I have an impression that in spite of the valuable material that has been brought before us in this discussion, we have not reached a decision on the problem that interests us. We are anxious above all to know how it becomes possible for the extra-ordinarily powerful life instinct to be overcome: whether this can only come about with the help of a disappointed libido or whether the ego can renounce its self-preservation for is own egoistic motives. It may be that we have failed to answer this psychological question because we have not adequate means of approaching it. We can, I think, only take as our starting-point the condition of melancholia, which is so familiar to us clinically, and a comparison between it and the affect of mourning. The affective processes in melancholia, however, and the vicissitudes undergone by the libido in that condition are totally unknown to us. Nor have we arrived as a psycho-analytic understanding of the chronic affect of mourning. Let us suspend our judgement until experience has solved this problem.[12]

The basic problem was how guilt, or anger, or any of the other psychological states could succeed in overcoming the power of the libido.

In the following years, Freud struggled for a better understanding of how this could be. This struggle resulted in the concepts of ego-splitting and the death instinct.

The ego is not a unitary element in the personality but is made up of "identifications," or better, "incorporations," of significant persons in the child's early life. Litman explains this complicated procedure in this way:

[12] Freud, *Works*, Vol. XI [1910], p. 232.

Energy withdrawn from a lost object is relocated in the ego and used to recreate the loved one as a permanent feature of the self, an *identification* of the ego with the abandoned object. "Thus, the shadow of the object fell upon the ego, and the latter could henceforth be judged by a special agency as though it were an object, the forsaken object." "Shadow" objects existing as structures in the ego (identifications) obviously are not fully integrated into the total personality. A demarcations zone, or fault line remains, along which ego splitting occurs.[13]

The concept of ego-splitting was refined by Freud in the 1920s when he identified the parts of the personality, which he called the id, ego and superego. The superego was one of the earliest splits of the ego and remains alive as an incorporation of certain parental attitudes. We are approved, loved, judged, condemned, condoned, abandoned, and forgiven by the superego. When this function is essentially negative, or when the ego has strong feelings of hostility against the superego, the state is set for possible suicide.

There are still many theoretical questions to be answered, as Litman points out: "For example, was it true that in most suicides the ego murdered the object? Or more often did the incorporated object murder the ego?" [14] Freud himself was not satisfied with the completeness of this explanation and, as he did so often, he looked to the future to provide a basis for improved understanding.

Early in his career, Freud embraced a monistic view of life. There was only one basic drive, the libido, which was

[13] Litman, in *Essays on Self-Destruction*, pp. 331-33.
[14] *Ibid.*, pp. 331-32.

life-affirming. Later, however, he abandoned this concept and:

> decided to assume the existence of only two basic instincts, Eros and the destructive instinct. The aim of the first of these basic instincts is to establish ever greater unities and to preserve them—thus, in short, to bind together; the aim of the second is, on the contrary, to undo connections and so to destroy things. In the case of the destructive instinct, we may suppose that its final aim is to lead what is living into an inorganic state. For this reason we call it the death instinct.[15]

As a medical man, Freud was aware of the twin processes of catabolism and anabolism—the contemporaneous build-up and break-down of the body cells. As a clinician, he was continually aware of the self-destructiveness of his patients. Although the neurotic is quick to blame external events of his problems, Freud saw through this defense and observed, "Their fate is for the most part arranged by themselves and determined by early infantile experience." [16] Enlarging on this observation, and bringing in the concept of the death instinct, he concluded that in human life as well as in the rest of nature. "Everything living dies from causes within itself." [17]

Although the death instinct, or thanatos, is a universally present force in all of life, it is seldom if ever seen in isolation. The two opposing drives are always joined. "The two kinds of instinct seldom—perhaps never—appear in isolation from each other, but are alloyed with each other

---

[15] Freud, *Works*, Vol. XXIII, pp. 148-59.
[16] Freud, *Beyond the Pleasure Principle* (New York: Bantam Books, [1920] 1959) , p. 44.
[17] *Ibid.*, p. 47.

in varying and very different proportions and so become unrecognizable to our judgment." [18]

The death instinct is the desire of the organism to escape from tension, the desire to return to the absolute peace of the inorganic state. It is the basis for all self-destructive behavior.

The concept of the death instinct has been received with varying attitudes by those follow in Freud's tradition. Norman O. Brown and Karl Menninger see it as a cornerstone of great importance, while Gregory Zilboorg accepts the concept as being valid but of little importance insofar as it "says nothing." [19]

The attempt here has been to present only the broadest survey of some of Freud's thinking as it relates to suicide. Suicide, as Freud recognized, is a complex action which has a multiplicity of motivation. There is no single dynamic that can account for man's tendency to kill himself. The concepts of ego-splitting and the death instinct are the main features of the phenomenon. Litman identifies these "specific suicide mechanisms" which Freud also identified:

(1) the loss of love objects, especially those who have loved in certain dangerous ways; (2) narcissistic injury, symbolically through failure or by direct physiological injury through fatigue or toxins; (3) overwhelming affect: rage, guilt, anxiety, or combinations; (4) extreme splitting of the ego with decathexis of most elements and a setting of one part

[18] Freud, *Civilization and Its Discontents* (New York: W. W. Norton, [1930] 1961), p. 66.

[19] Brown, *Life Against Death* (New York: Random House, 1959); Menninger, *Man Against Himself* (New York: Harcourt Brace Jovanovich, 1938); Zilboorg, "Considerations on Suicide with Particular Reference to That of the Young," *American Journal of Orthopsychiatry*, 8 (January 1937), 15.

against the rest; and (5) a special attitude and plan, often based on an identification with someone who was suicidal.[20]

After expressing his basic agreement with the Freudian concepts of suicide, Litman makes this observation out of his experience working with suicidal persons:

> The suicidal drama often reproduces not so much guilt for the unconscious wish of the child to murder the parent but rather a reaction of abandonment on the part of the child to the parent's unconscious wish for the child's death. The mechanism of regression and the themes in suicide of helplessness, constriction, and paranoid distrust have made the deepest impression on me.[21]

Freud used the oedipal drama as the organizing point for many of his most important theoretical constructs. Litman, however, finds the pre-oedipal position more helpful in understanding suicidal behavior:

> At the Suicide Prevention Center, I am more accustomed to using the mother-child, preoedipal relationship as a reference concept. Further research, hopefully, will clarify this issue.
> It is remarkable that Freud said so litle about the all-important attitude of the mother in instilling into a child the desire for life. It is remarkable because Freud was well aware of the influence of his own mother in instilling into him a feeling of confidence and a zest for living. Moreover, he has found in his patients and in himself, as a reason for continuing to live, the idea that his premature death would be painful to his mother. When Freud's mother died in

[20] Litman, in *Essays on Self-Destruction,* p. 338.
[21] *Ibid.,* p. 340.

1930, aged 95, Freud noticed in himself a feeling of liberation. "I was not allowed to die as long as she was alive, and now I may." [22]

Freudian thinking did not stop with Freud's death. He left behind him several dedicated disciples who continue to express and develop his ideas. Two of them are Fenichel and Menninger.

Otto Fenichel accepts without reservation the ideas of Freud concerning suicide.[23] He supports the concept that basically suicide is the murder of someone else turned in upon the would-be murderer—what Shneidman has called "murder in the 180th degree." [24] Fenichel also stresses the conflict between the ego and the superego as the underlying dynamic. Neurotically depressed persons are the most likely to suicide, since the dynamics of depression are similar to those of suicide. A punitive superego angrily punishes the ego: "An ambivalent dependence on a sadistic superego and the necessity to get rid of an unbearable guilt tension at any cost are the most frequent causes of suicide." [25]

In contrast to depression, a compulsion neurosis does not often lead to suicide. The libido of the person is not totally involved in the conflict between the ego and superego. Because the compulsive is actually expressing so much aggression against the object, he does not need to turn so much against himself.

If Fenichel stresses the Freudian concept of ego-splitting

[22] *Ibid.*, p. 340.
[23] Fenichel, *The Psychoanalytic Theory of Neurosis* (New York: W. W. Norton, 1945).
[24] Shneidman, in *The Study of Lives*, p. 204.
[25] Fenichel, *Psychoanalytic Theory*, p. 294.

in understanding suicidal behavior, Menninger lays emphasis on the death instinct.

The death instinct is a universal human fact, according to Menninger, and we must come to understand it better so that we can have some control over it. "We have come to see that just as the child must learn to love wisely, so he must learn to hate expeditiously, to turn destructive tendencies away from himself toward enemies that actually threaten him rather than toward the friendly and the defenseless, the more usual victims of destructive energy." [26]

But this is not to say that we can ever avoid the death instinct. "It is true, nevertheless, that in the end each man kills himself in his own selected way, fast or slow, soon or late." [27]

Menninger holds that there are three basic motivations for suicidal behavior, the wish to kill, the wish to be killed, and the wish to die. The motivation of the first is aggression, the second is guilt, and the third is the wish for peace. The motivations are usually interrelated, just as the first is aggression, the second is guilt, and the third is the wish for peace. The motivations are usually interrelated, just as the two basic drives, eros and thanatos, are interrelated.

Suicidal behavior can be seen in four forms: the acute, which refers to the overt suicidal attempt; the chronic, the slow, steady, lifelong "suicide by inches"; focal, the localized attack on parts of the body; and organic, which can be described as the psychosomatic illness. All are expressions of thanatos, and involve, in varying proportions, the three death wishes named above.

[26] Menninger, *Man Against Himself*, p. vii.
[27] *Ibid.*, p. vii.

To combat these forms of self-destructiveness, Menninger urges the mobilization of intellect:

> I believe that our best defense against self-destructiveness lies in the courageous application of intelligence to human phenomenology. If such is our nature, it were better that we knew it and knew it in all its protean manifestations. To see all forms of self-destruction from the standpoint of their dominant principles would seem to be the logical progress toward self-preservation and toward a unified view of medical science.[28]

In addition to those who follow directly the Freudian tradition, other theorists have sought explanations of suicidal behavior. The best survey of these other schools of thought is found in *The Cry for Help*, by Norman Farberow and Edwin Shneidman.[29] We now turn to a brief survey of the contributions of some of these theories.

Jung

The Jungian point of view on suicide, as expressed by Klopfer, stresses the concept of the separation of the ego from the true self. The ego, in this framework, is "merely the center of the conscious part of our personality functioning."[30] The self constitutes a deeper center of the functioning of the individual organism, maintaining the contact between the individual and the cosmos to which it belongs.

To experience life as meaningful, there must be at least some contact between the ego and the self. When the separation widens, a sense of meaninglessness and futility en-

[28] *Ibid.,* vii.
[29] New York: McGraw-Hill, 1961.
[30] *Ibid.,* p. 193.

sues. In an unconscious effort to remedy this situation, the ego may want to die in order to return to the archetype of the *magna mater*—to regain constant contact with the self—and to be reborn. Suicide may be the way that this is attempted. This striving for rebirth is a major Jungian concept.

Another important concept in regard to suicide is Jung's formulation of the dark and light side of the self. When the dark side predominates, death may be seen as preferable to life, and suicide becomes an active possibility. We see this condition in (1) the death of a hero or martyr, where the "life of the individual seems less important than the preservation of the ideal"; (2) cases of great pain or mental anguish when death is seen as a liberation; (3) counterphobic reaction to death; (4) the desire for reunion with a dead loved one; (5) the search for freedom; and (6) the search for closure.

Phenomenologically considered, there four classifications of suicide according to the Jungian conception. These classifications are polar in nature. The first is the pole of collective and individual suicide which refers to the distinction of whether the suicidal act is in obedience to, or in contradiction of, the cultural expectation. The second class designates the poles of active and passive suicide, the latter referring to a situation where a person may save himself from death but does not take the action necessary, such as in the case of a captain going down with his ship. The third polar pair is that of the sincere and the attention-getting suicide attempts which are distinguished in reference to the wish to die. The final class is the planned and the impulsive suicide.

Adler

The Adlerian understanding of suicide centers around four concepts which are basic to an understanding of Adler's theory of personality.[31]

The doctrine of a pampered life-style is seen as useful in describing some instances of suicide. One who has a pampered life-style is a dependent person who always tries to lean on others and who is incapable of working with other people on the basis of equality. He is characterized by deficient social interest (another basic Adlerian concept), and his only major expectation in life is that others will fulfill his wishes. When this style of living fails, he has few personal resources to fall back on and may become suicidal.

The suicidal person may have strong feelings of inferiority which he seeks to compensate for by great attempts to achieve positions of great importance. He tends to be ambitious and vain, and because his self-expectations are unrealistic in relation to his abilities, he is apt to fail. When this happens his feelings of inferiority are frequently exposed, and he may attempt suicide.

Adler also observes that the level of activity among suicides is high, tending toward mania. They frequently act in an uncontrolled manner.

Finally, Adler points out that the life-style of a suicidal person is characterized by veiled aggression. It is not unusual that he seeks to hurt others by hurting himself and then looking for sympathy. This method of handling aggression may easily become suicidal.

[31] *Ibid.*, p. 204.

Sullivan

Sullivan's concept of personality stresses the importance of interaction between persons. The attitudes of significant other people are of prime importance in the development of the personality. A person's self-image is largely derived from the introjections of what others communicate to him about himself.

According to Sullivan, a person's response to a situation is a response of the whole person, and isolated personality factors are not understood unless they are seen in the context of the full personality.

Sullivan would stress that the response of suicide is a complex reaction, and one that cannot be simply explained. However, some generalizations can be made. Suicidal behavior implies "hateful and hostile types of integrations with other persons." [32] It includes the elements of anxiety, the products of inadequate personifications; envy, stemming from a lack of a sense of one's own worth; and depression, which points to self-deprecating thoughts.

Horney

The Horney conceptualization of suicidal behavior centers around the four main factors: the feelings of hopelessness, suffering, alienation, and the search for glory.[33]

Suicide, according to Horney, is an attempt of the individual to deal with these feelings of inadequacy. She stresses, too, childhood development and the attitudes of the significant others in the child's environment. Also to be considered in the study of suicide are the elements of the cultural mores, values of life, and concepts of life and death.

[32] *Ibid.*, p. 220.
[33] *Ibid.*, p. 236.

Kelly

The personal construct theory of personality, as expressed by Kelly, asks the basic question: "What was the person trying to validate by his (suicidal) action?" [34]

In order to understand any specific incident of suicide, we must understand the individual person's construction of life. Specifically, this school of thought looks to (1) the basic postulate and choice corollary by which this person lives; (2) dilating versus constriction—whether the person is expanding or narrowing his life in order to make some sense of it; (3) the role of anxiety; (4) the person's percepting of threat; (5) hostility; and (6) guilt.

In his overview and summary of these positions, Norman Farberow finds that five elements appear to be commonly discussed by advocates of the different points of view:

1. Dependency is commonly seen as an important factor in suicidal behavior. When a person has not gained sufficient personal independence and integration, he is at the mercy of external factors and has not the inner strength to handle constructively, stressful situations.

2. Aggression and hostility are terms that were often used interchangeably and are frequently seen as primary considerations in any expression of self-destructive behavior.

3. Guilt appears to play an important role in a person's decision to kill himself.

4. Anxiety is a broad term, and although some of the schools do not talk about it explicitly it appears to be a concept that is implicitly considered in most attempts to understand suicide.

[34] *Ibid.,* p. 255.

5. Finally, suicide is often understood in terms of an individual's attempt to make an adjustment either to himself or to his environment.[35]

As might be expected, the attempts to explain the dynamics of suicide appear to rest on the theoretical formulations of personality as they are understood by the particular schools. It is extremely difficult, if not impossible, to speak of a psychology of suicide. Although there is some overlapping of concepts, and much common ground between the schools, the basic orientation of the individual theorist will largely determine his understanding of the dynamics of suicidal behavior.

The best we can do at this point is to return to the conclusion that Freud made that suicidal behavior has a multiplicity of motivations and appears to be best understood in terms of the specific person who is suicidal. The meanings of the act (conscious or unconscious) are best understood in terms of the individual personality structure. With Freud, we look to the future for more understanding of this complex issue.

---

[35] *Ibid.*, p. 290.

Chapter 3
Preventing Suicide

Most suicides can be prevented. This is especially true for that type of suicide that is represented by Dr. Murphy, Mrs. Lloyd, and Johnny. These are relatively stable people who are experiencing some misfortune, are temporarily overwhelmed by intensive feelings, and who are suffering a temporary failure in their ability to cope. Nearly all of such suicides could be prevented if the significant people around them were able to recognize the suicidal crisis and respond to it in a helpful and supportive way. Short-term, active, crisis intervention is nearly always effective for such people. Anyone in the emotional vicinity of the suicidal person, including family members, clergymen, physicians, therapists, and friends is in a key position to prevent a tragic and wasteful death.

Another type of suicidal person is represented by Anita, June, and Mr. Harris. Less stable emotionally, and having fewer long-term, supportive social relationships, these people live in the gray area of life. Never far from suicidal behavior, their life-style includes frequent thoughts of death as a way out, many suicide attempts, a chronic lack of helpful resources, and a generally maladaptive life-style. Included in this type are alcoholics, compulsive gamblers, homosexuals, malignant masochists, harlequins, failing psychopaths, and other types of character disorders and certain psychoses.

If suicidal at all, these people are perpetually dangerous suicide risks and will often resolve one suicidal crisis only to be on the brink of the next. The long-term prognosis is less optimistic for them than for the more stable group who will usually emerge from a suicidal crisis in a healthy and adaptive way.

But in both cases, the incident of suicide can be dramatically lowered and many lives saved if those who are in touch with suicidal persons can learn to recognize, evaluate, and intervene effectively into the crisis.

Communication

Mr. Andrews had called his priest to say goodbye. He wanted Father Patrick to know that these last three years during which he had attended Father Patrick's church had been the most significant years of his life. It was with deep regret, he said, that it was necessary for him to return now to Chicago since he had enjoyed his life in Los Angeles so much. He wanted Father Patrick to know that he felt that the priest was one of the most helpful and understanding men he had ever met and that he would miss him. Father Patrick responded to this expression of gratitude in an appreciative way and hoped that things would go well for him. The men were about ready to hang up when Mr. Andrews had another request. "Oh, by the way, Father, I just wanted to ask that in case anything should happen, not that it will, you understand, but in case it should, you're the one I would want to conduct my funeral and I wonder if you would be willing to do this." The request sounded a little strange coming from a forty-one-year-old, apparently healthy man, but Father Patrick acquiesced and said that, although he was sure the need would not arise in the near future, he would be pleased to be available. The call was then terminated cordially.

The conversation stuck in Father Patrick's mind, and he began thinking about Mr. Andrews. He hadn't really known him all that well and was a little surprised at the intensity of the farewell. He tried to bring more clearly into focus just who Mr. Andrews was, and the picture that emerged was that of a relatively quiet, almost withdrawn man, always with a gentle, bashful smile. He would stand around rather awkwardly after services and after church dinners waiting for someone to speak to him and respond to any overture in an overeager, possessive way. He was obviously, now that Father Patrick thought about it, a man hungry for human contact and overly grateful for any small bit that one would give him.

Father Patrick's mind now returned to the telephone conversation and the strange request about the funeral which had struck him as being out of context, and he began to have strange feelings about it. Still, many people like to think ahead, and many priests and ministers are approached with similar requests; perhaps he was reading in or over-reacting, but the more he thought about it, the more Father Patrick realized that he couldn't simply let it go; something was bothering him and it had to do with Mr. Andrews and his talk about the funeral. Putting aside the work that he was doing, Father Patrick paid a call on this man. During the course of the ensuing conversation, Mr. Andrews tearfully admitted to Father Patrick that he was planning to drive the car over a cliff and commit suicide on his drive back to Chicago. Because Father Patrick was the kind of priest who was observant and responsive to his own feelings a human life was probably saved.

Many people who are contemplating suicide, being ambivalent, communicate their intention to other people. Recognition of these communications is the first important step in effective suicide prevention. Prior to his death, Johnny made several public announcements of his intention to kill himself that night. He showed his friends the pills he was to take and asked them on several occasions if they thought that there were enough to do the job. He also called his girlfriend and told her what he intended to do. He then made enough noise at home in the middle of the night to awaken his mother, as a last attempt at communication. Mrs. Lloyd was communicating enough clues to alarm her daughter several months before her death, and Dr. Murphy tried to tell his pastor in subtle ways that he was nearing the end of his rope on that fateful Saturday. Unfortunately for these people, their communications went unrecognized and no response was forthcoming.

Another case will illustrate other attempts of a suicidal person to communicate and ask for help. After Mr. Rogers' suicidal death, everyone said that this forty-three-year-old successful engineer was the last person anyone would expect to have killed himself. He was a stable person, who had been happily married to the same woman for twenty years. He was successful in his work, having attained a supervisory position with a minimum of formal education.

He was described by his wife as being frequently nervous and jittery, and as having trouble sleeping. During these times he would become withdrawn and read obsessively. Sometimes he would not talk for days at a time, then he would come out of his mood and be normal. He had many interests in addition to his reading. He was an avid sports fan, and he enjoyed taking vacations with his wife when they would travel by auto across the country.

He had been having some problems with drinking but had seen a physician about three months prior to his death, received a prescription, and the drinking stopped entirely. Everyone was shocked when he was discovered at his home by his wife on a Monday afternoon dead of a self-inflicted gunshot wound. Investigation of the case, however, revealed that there had been many communications that Mr. Rogers had been sending out in the months and weeks prior to his death, none of which were correctly interpreted by those close to him.

The beginning of the current stress situation was the introduction into his office of a new computer which Mr. Rogers felt might be above his ability to comprehend. He had some fears that in time it might even replace him. He had expressed fears to several people including his boss and had been reassured that his job situation was very secure. The company had always been well pleased with his performance. These reassurances failed to make him feel better, however, and the insecurity spread into other areas of his life. He told a friend at one time that he didn't know what he would ever do if his wife were to leave him. This fear also had no basis in fact.

Two and a half weeks prior to his death, a friend recalled, Mr. Rogers had told at lunch how much he appreciated having a good friend, someone that he could tell his troubles to and confide in. The friend was puzzled by this expression of gratitude, since Mr. Rogers was not the type to confide in anyone, and since he did not know what to make of this statement, he simply decided to drop it. About two days after that, Mr. Rogers asked for an appointment with his boss and thanked him for being "the best boss that he had ever worked for," and told him how much he appreciated working for such a man. Mr. Rogers' boss was puzzled by the conversation and remembers making a comment at the time that it seemed like a farewell speech, but he never inquired further. Two days before his death, Mr. Rogers borrowed a gun from one of the men whom he supervised at work, giving the excuse that he was concerned about burglars in his neighborhood. There had, in fact, been no reports of burglars in the neighborhood, and it was this gun that Mr. Rogers used to kill himself.

In regard to his prior suicidal behavior, his wife said that he had never made a suicide attempt before. However, she then went on to relate that six years earlier he had to have his stomach pumped because of an overdose of barbiturates. The incident was passed off as an accident because it happened in conjunction with too much drinking. Three years after that, Mr. Rogers was found unconscious in his car in his garage with the motor running. Had he not been rescued at this time, he might very well have died from carbon monoxide, and again the incident was passed off as an accident. In each of these incidents Mr. Rogers was attempting to communicate his growing distress and his diminishing ability to cope with strong feelings of insecurity and unworthiness. The growing depression was undiagnosed, however, because it simply wasn't recognized by those who were in contact with him.

This pattern is true with most suicidal deaths. Careful investigation after a suicide usually reveals many clear incidents of attempts at communication by the suicide victim which have been missed or ignored or misinterpreted by those close to him.

Why should this be, that communications which are so clear in retrospect are so often missed or ignored at the time that they are given? The main cause of ignored suicidal communication is the presence of anxiety on the part of the listener. Most people don't want to hear the clues to suicide because the very topic makes them uncomfortable. This is especially true if the suicidal person is someone for whom they feel a responsibility—a family member, a friend, or colleague. To know that someone you care about is feeling suicidal and may actually be considering killing himself, usually produces in the listener the negative feelings of being rejected, being unimportant, powerless, unneeded, and unwanted. In addition, some people feel that the presence of suicidal ideation has some weird or other-worldly, spooky cause behind it, and the tendency is to flee from involvement in this kind of uncomfortable situation. As a result, they will employ a variety of psychological defenses to separate themselves and so avoid the unpleasant feelings.

Sometimes they will repress the communication, that is, actually not hear the words being articulated, and they will be unable to recall them even after a death has occurred.

Another common psychological defense is that of denial. The listener will hear the words and be able to recall them later, but will deny that they had any meaning or significance. Examples of denial are the boss who commented that Mr. Rogers was making a farewell speech but could not see that it had any significance. The same kind of denial was in effect when Mrs. Rogers could relate two previous suicide attempts, which might easily have proved fatal to her husband, and at the same time deny that they had any meaning and be genuinely surprised when a few years later her husband actually killed himself.

A third psychological defense that people frequently use is that of rationalization. In response to a definite suicidal threat, they will say something like, "You don't really mean that," which evaluation has no basis in fact whatsoever except in the listener's own anxiety. Mrs. Lloyd's husband, when confronted directly by his daughter's concern about his wife, rationalized it away in terms of his daughter's overreacting when in fact she was not.

A fourth way people manifest anxiety when being exposed to suicidal communication is by reacting aggressively. Many people will become angry upon hearing a suicidal hint or threat, as if to say the suicidal victim has no right in exposing the listener to such feelings of anxiety and discomfort.

In other situations, people are aware of the suicidal communication and are concerned, but are immobilized. Sometimes this immobilization stems from a fear of invading the other person's privacy, and this fear of intruding makes it difficult for them to respond openly. Still others feel that to talk about suicide to a suicidal person would be to encourage them to carry out their plan of death. Research and experience have proved that both fears are unfounded in reality. The reason that a suicidal person is making his communication is for the purpose of inviting concern and inquiry into the state of his life, and if this concern is not manifested, the suicidal person experiences this as a rejection and as a lack of caring. The normal effect of this is to encourage him in his suicidal thinking. People are not driven to suicide by a caring inquiry as to whether or not they are suicidal. They may well be driven to suicide by an avoidance of the topic on the part of the listener from whom they are wanting a concerned response.

Another fear that holds some people back from recognizing and responding to suicidal communication is a fear of getting too involved. Some people don't want the responsibility of helping another person stay alive, and they try to avoid the cry for help. Most suicidal crises are relatively short-lived, and when a suicidal person is asking for help, he does not need a lifelong commitment, but only the willingness from a concerned person to become actively involved for a short period of time. It seems like a small price to ask if a life can be saved.

There are other reasons, however, why some suicidal communications are not observed. Some chronically suicidal people place themselves in the position of the shepherd boy who cried wolf too often. Even when he is surrounded by concerned people who would like to be of help, crying suicide too often has the effect of minimizing its importance in the minds of those significant other people, and soon the cries are not taken seriously. More than one life has been lost because the suicidal person too often used the cry as a way of manipulation, and thus found ears around him desensitized when a true suicidal crisis developed.

Some suicidal people who have major problems with feelings of powerlessness and being ineffectual have found suicidal threats to be a potent blackmail force by which they can intimidate well-meaning people around them. The listener is caught in the unacceptable double-bind of being manipulated in an autocratic way or being made to feel responsible for another person's death. This kind of emotional blackmail usually results in feelings of intense anger and resentment toward the suicidal person which may be satisfying to him in the short run, but ultimately results in alienation and usually in becoming more seriously suicidal in the future.

These are some of the major reasons then why suicidal communications so often go unheeded and even unheard. Sometimes the simple lack of information that suicidal communications are usually an integral part of the build-up toward self-death will result in the communications not being taken seriously. The facts are, of course, that most people who kill themselves have given communication of their intention to do so prior to their attempt. The two basic concepts of ambivalence and the communication nature of the entire suicidal action are fundamental and provide a major opportunity for the prevention of suicide.

Evaluation

Once it has become apparent that a suicidal situation exists it becomes necessary to make an evaluation of the suicidal danger. Although the vast majority of committed suicides have given previous hints and warnings of their intention to kill themselves, not all people who make suicidal communications will go on to die. At the Suicide Prevention Center in Los Angeles, only about fifteen percent of the nine thousand calls that the center receives annually are rated as high suicide risks. The remaining eighty-five percent are people who are low or moderate suicide risks, who are unhappy, depressed, and needy people. Such people deserve to be helped, but short-term crisis and suicide intervention is often not appropriate. Since suicide prevention has certain characteristics that are unique, it is important that the counselor or clergyman be able to recognize a high suicide risk when he meets one. He should have at his disposal the criteria by which he is able to make an accurate judgment as to how high a suicide risk this particular counselee represents. This evaluation will then determine what kind of counseling response he will make. There are three basic areas of evaluation which can help the counselor to make the important distinction between a high, medium, and low suicide risk. These are: the demographics of suicide, the dynamics of the suicidal decision, and the determination to suicide.

The Demographics of Suicide

In chapter 2, a statistical description of people who kill themselves was presented. Some of the important findings that are reported in that chapter include the fact that men kill themselves at about twice the frequency of women. It was also reported there that women tend to make about twice as many suicide attempts as men. Although these, like all statistics, can only present the overall general nature of suicidal behavior and are not sensitive to the dynamics of individual people, nevertheless the sex of the person is an important variable and can give the observer an early first clue about the lethality of the counselee. When this fact is taken in conjunction with other information it offers an important dimension to the recognition of highly lethal persons.

The fact that men kill themselves twice as often with

only half as many suicide attempts is indicative of the fact that men tend to use more highly lethal means of attempting suicide and that they are less prone to make suicide attempts in an effort to demonstrate their unhappiness. When the counselor is speaking with a man, therefore, who is communicating some suicidal intention, the statistics say that he is more likely to be dealing with someone who will go on and kill himsef as opposed to someone who may make a low lethal attempt as a means of calling attention to his desperate feelings.

A second major finding of the statistical study of suicided persons is the importance of the variable of age. Suicide in the subteen years is so rare as to be statistically insignificant. In adolescence, the suicide rate is very low but continues to rise with age. The most lethal age group in our culture is comprised of people over sixty.

Most clergymen have had experiences with young people thinking, threatening, and even attempting suicide. By such behavior these young people are normally seeking to draw attention to themselves and to their situation, which they feel is getting beyond their ability to cope. Such young people deserve a warm and concerned response, but as a group they represent a relatively low suicidal risk, and the clergyman can feel relatively safe that if he makes a caring response and takes the young person's plight seriously, the chance of a suicide is unlikely. This cannot be said, however, if the person making the suicidal communication is an older person. Such people may be slower to make suicidal communications than their adolescent counterparts, and when they do, it normally menas that the likelihood of their actually killing themselves is much higher. Such people will usually need more than a concerned and warm response from their counselor. They will need action in the form of some change in their situation.

The statistics of certain special situations can be very helpful to the practicing clergyman in an attempt to gain the first clues about a highly suicidal situation. The suicide rate of divorced males, for example, in Los Angeles County reaches the dramatic figure of 152 per one thousand population. This figure is so high that any divorced male who is communicating suicidal ideas must be taken very seriously —almost regardless of other kinds of information.

As a tool for evaluating suicidal risk, suicide statistics have certain limitations. Like all statistics, they report only general trends and overall characteristics. Any careful evaluation of suicide potential must include much more than that, but an awareness of the general characteristics over the population provide a good place to begin to understand the individual counselee.

The Dynamics of the Decision

The decision to kill oneself is, in most cases, not a sudden one, but has developmental history which often covers months and even years. The further along the counselee is in this decision-making process the more serious is his suicide potential. An understanding of the dynamics of this decision-making process is of great value for the counselor since it is important to know where his counselee is in the process of making this decision. There are two factors which interact in this area:

1. *Stress.* The dynamics of the decision-making process as it moves toward suicide usually begin with the introduction of stress. This stress can be either some event which is distasteful to the person and which he is going to have dif-

ficulty in handling, or it can come about as the result of normal development, such as the beginning of puberty, menopause, or the advent of old age.

Sometimes the event can be clearly understood as having monumental implications for the person that it affects. Many men who had their fortunes entirely wrapped up in the stock market on Black Friday, 1929, and who watched the crash of the market on that day, reacted to that stress by jumping from tall buildings on Wall Street. People can often understand the shock effect and the gravity of the stress which led some of these men to feel that there was nothing left for them. Other times, however, the stress is much more subtle and is not normally thought of as being so severe as to produce even suicidal ideas, let alone suicidal actions. When Johnny went to pick up Susan for his date on that Saturday night and found that she had stood him up again, it was an event that produced enough stress that he ended killing himself. Although most people would not react that way, for Johnny, at this time, it was a significant stress. In order to be correctly evaluated, therefore, stress should be seen not only in terms of the severity of the event, but also in terms of what the event meant to the person who experienced it. One way to determine this is by observing the individual's reaction to the stress, that is, the symptoms that he is manifesting.

People normally respond to the stress of loss by becoming reactively depressed. The intensity of the depression, however, is an important variable that the counselor will want to take carefully into consideration. How depressed does the counselee appear? Is he just feeling a little blue, down in the mouth for a short period of time, and generally unhappy; or does he have all the classical symptoms of a deep depression, including inability to sleep (or inability to get out of bed), a loss of appetite and sexual interest, a slowdown in his ability to speak and to move, and general withdrawal from people? Is he becoming ruminative and locked into the depression?

Another common symptom of stress is confusion, and again, the degree and the intensity of the confusion must be carefully watched. Is the person experiencing a flood of ideas and alternatives that he is unable to separate and to distinguish for a short time, or is the confusion so deep that he finds it impossible to articulate clearly—perhaps even forgetting who he is or where he is, and being uncertain about what is happening to him?

Another possible stress reaction is denial. Sometimes in response to a severe stress where one would normally expect an individual to have a reaction of depression or confusion, the individual appears totally calm and serene as if nothing serious had happened. Such a reaction is usually a bad sign, and if the individual is also making suicidal communications, in a calm manner, this can be an extremely dangerous sign.

The first major phase in the dynamics of a decision toward suicide is the introduction of some stress event. The symptomatic reaction that the individual has to the stress is the second important consideration. Generally speaking, the more severe the stress and the more intense the symptoms, the higher the suicidal potential. But neither stress nor the reaction to stress can be meaningfully interpreted without balancing it with the next consideration in the dynamics of the decision, which is the individual's coping abiltiy.

2. *Coping Ability.* A person who has the ego strength to

cope well can usually handle a great amount of stress and manifest intense symptoms with no significant suicidal danger. A person who does not have strong coping ability, however, can be thrown into a serious suicidal crisis by a relatively mild stress. The ability to cope, therefore, is an important dimension of the dynamics of the suicidal decision and it consists of two major factors: internal ego strength and the employment of external resources.

The internal ego strength includes one's ability to conceptualize stress in a realistic way, to keep meaningful and realistic perspective on feelings of guilt, shame, and fear, and to organize one's time and emotional strength in an appropriate and creative way. Internal coping strength can usually be judged by the individual's personal history. Normally, a stable person who is able to maintain some intimate and long-term relationships, who has a personal history which flows purposely toward some socially acceptable goal, who is able to accept responsibility for his own behavior and the welfare of those in his immediate emotional life can be assumed to have a relatively strong internal coping strength.

Weak internal coping ability is normally characterized by a chaotic life-style, short-term, unsatisfying personal relationships, a history of suicide attempts, psychiatric or frequent medical hospitalization, or a life-style which includes excessive use of alcohol, narcotics, gambling, or promiscuity. These are the signs that the individual has a difficult time tolerating stress and anxiety, and he prefers acting out impulsively to the alternative of working out problems in a stable and constructive way. Persons with weak internal coping ability, especially when there is a history of suicide attempts, present high suicidal danger when any significant stress is introduced into their life-style.

The second facet of any individual's ability to cope is the way in which he is able to employ his external resources. External resources include any sources of strength that lie outside of the individual's own personality structure. Significant other people, social contacts, money, professional people, friends, all represent external resources. One of the most serious signs of a highly suicidal situation is a person who has no external resources. This is one of the reasons that elderly people present such high suicide rates. Their external resources are often at a minimum; friends and family members having either died or moved away, their health may be failing, their physical mobility severely restricted. Older people are often placed in a nursing-home situation where their physical needs may be taken care of but the emotional environment is sterile and basically uncaring. Such people have a difficult time mobilizing external resources simply because there are so few external resources to mobilize, and when they experience a stress which is beyond their internal ability to cope there is no place else to go. This is the reason, too, why divorced males represent such a high suicide risk. One of their main external resources, that is the wife, is not there and cannot be called on in any crisis. The presence of external resources is therefore one of the major dominants of the severity of suicide risk.

The simple existence, however, of adequate resources is no guarantee that they will be affective in a suicidal crisis. The suicidal person's acceptance of these resources as well as the resources' willingness to respond are critical dimensions. Mr. Rogers, for example, was a successful supervising engineer in his corporation. He was surrounded by good resources, including his wife, his boss, his company, and some friends. Mr. Rogers, however, represented a certain large class of American males, who are simply, by their personality structure, incapable of letting significant other people know of their distress and ask for help. Such people live as if they had no resources whatsoever and in large measure are just as bad off as the skid-row alcoholic, who literally has no resources to mobilize.

Another example is the suicidal adolescent, who, although living in a close-knit family, refuses to permit his parents to be informed about his desperate suicidal feelings because of real or fantasied fear that they would be rejecting of these painful, delicate, vulnerable feelings.

In our culture, generally speaking, women seem to suffer less from this inability to accept the help of significant external resources than men. Some women, however, lean on their resources so heavily and so often that the resources themselves become exhausted and rejecting and are no longer helpfully available.

Suicide risk rises with the disappearance or unavailability of resources. A person with many resources easily available to him normally represents a relatively low suicide risk.

The dynamics of the decision to suicide, then, can be accurately determined when one observes how stress and coping ability merge. Neither is complete without the other, and a rough graph of the interaction might be drawn as in figure 1. The stronger the person's ability to cope, the more stress he will be able to handle without becoming seriously suicidal. A person with weak coping ability, that is, one who suffers an inability both in internal coping and in mobilizing external resources for himself may easily be thrown into a severe suicidal crisis with a relatively small amount of stress.

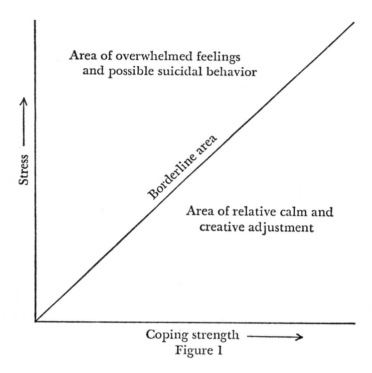

Figure 1

Suicide usually represents a person's way out of a situation of painful stress with which he is unable to cope. In some people, however, June, for example, suicide represents a way of coping, and she will become suicidal almost immediately upon the introduction of any stress. Such people represent a chronically high suicidal risk since suicide is written into their basic style of life.

The interaction between stress and coping ability, then,

represents the major dynamics of the decision to suicide and offers an important measure of suicide potential.

The Determination to Suicide

Probably the single, most clear criterion of suicidal danger comes by evaluating the person's determination toward suicide as it is manifested in his suicidal plan. People usually do not kill themselves impulsively or meaninglessly or without considerable forethought and planning. The determination to suicide usually takes a specific form, the details of which have been carefully worked out. A careful analysis of the suicidal person's plan, therefore, presents the most accurate way of assessing his immediate suicidal danger. There are three major facets of any suicide plan: (1) the specificity of the means; (2) the lethality of the means; and (3) the availability of the means.

1. *Specificity*. A highly suicidal person knows exactly what means he will employ to kill himself. In the absence of this specific knowledge, the assumption can be made that the suicide risk is probably not high. Most people who plan to kill themselves have already decided that it will either be by a gun, by a knife, by pills, by jumping, etc. More than that, if they are far along in the development of their plan they will know which gun, which knife, which ledge they will employ to destroy themselves. So dedicated do they become to the specific means of death that if one particular means is taken from them or made unavailable, they usually will not move immediately to an alternative means of suicide. It is important, then, for the counselor if he is confronting a person he suspects of being suicidal, to ask him the direct question—"How do you plan to kill yourself?" —and then listen very carefully for the answer. If the person

replies generally, "Well, I don't really know; maybe I'll shoot myself," or "I really hadn't thought much about it —perhaps sleeping pills," the chances are that this person does not represent an immediately high suicide risk.

2. *Lethality.* The second criterion is the lethality of the suicidal means. If in answer to the question, "How do you plan to kill yourself," the patient replies, in common with some adolescents, "Oh, I'll probably take a half a bottle of aspirin tablets," or some other means which is clearly not lethal, the person does not represent an immediately high suicide risk. It is also very hard to kill one's self by cutting, traffic accident, or performing some action in a crowd, where the likelihood of his being rescued is high. On the other hand, guns or jumping represent very lethal means of suicide in that they are deadly, and they provide little time for rescue. Even a high overdose of barbiturates still leaves provision for rescue in that it takes several hours after the ingestion of the pills for life to cease. During this time, most people can be saved with proper medical treatment.

3. *Availability.* The third criterion of a suicidal plan is availability of the means. Even if one is planning to kill himself by shooting himself in the head with a gun, certainly a specific and lethal means of death, if the gun that he is planning to use is not immediately available to him, this has a mitigating effect upon the suicide rating. If he has not purchased a gun, or he knows about a specific gun but it's in someone else's house, or he doesn't know its exact location; this has quite a different meaning than if the gun is so available that it is, at the moment, sitting on his table already loaded. For one thing, the unavailability of the means provides more time for rescue, and secondly,

it indicates that the person has not quite yet progressed to a total determination to suicide.

Anyone who is communicating suicidal thoughts or ideas needs help. The importance of rating the immediate suicidal danger is useful in determining what kind of help and with what urgency it must be delivered.

Intervention

Suicide prevention can be carried on on many different levels and in many different forms. What is appropriate depends entirely on the evaluation of the suicide potential. It depends on how far a suicidal person has progressed in his determination to kill himself.

The first level, the most extreme point, in this progress toward determination is when the person has already taken some physical action of self-destruction. It is the point when Dr. Murphy, Mrs. Lloyd, and Johnny have already ingested the pills and are lying down to die. It is the point where Mr. Harris turns the loaded gun upon himself and is beginning to apply pressure to the trigger. At this level, there exists a physical emergency and appropriate suicide intervention is direct physical action. The overdose victim needs to be treated medically, and soon, and the only question left is one of tactics; how that aid can most efficiently be delivered to the victim. It is not infrequent that a suicidal person will take a lethal overdose of some barbiturate and refuse to cooperate in his own rescue. In such a situation, the would-be rescuer has the choice of attempting to physically force medical care on the victim, or to wait until the victim loses consciousness and then provide him with the needed treatment. This latter course is often the preferable one.

At such a time, what is needed are resource people who are capable of recognizing that a physical, medical emergency exists and capable of responding to it in such a way that the help is efficiently delivered. Once the victim is out of physical danger the immediate suicidal crisis is usually passed. The suicide has temporarily been prevented and the way is open for appropriate follow-up action.

The second level of suicide intervention occurs when the victim has not yet taken any physical action to harm himself, but he has clearly determined to do so and has created a carefully thought out suicidal plan which bears the dangerous characteristics of lethality, specificity, and availability. Sometimes physical action is required at this level too. As was discussed above, most suicidal people, once they have carefully thought out the means by which they plan to kill themselves, will not digress from this plan and will not easily substitute alternate methods. It is often advisable, therefore, that the gun, the too-available pills, or whatever other means have been decided on, be confiscated and taken out of reach of the victim. In addition, careful plans should be made to insure that the suicidal person not be left alone throughout the duration of the crisis. The important people in his own life's sphere should be alerted and informed of the seriousness of the danger. The cry for help which the suicidal person is attempting to articulate should be amplified by every means possible, and all appropriate people should be enlisted to form a protective web around him.

Many people, who find themselves suddenly placed in the

position of having to take some responsibility for another person's impending suicide, balk at taking the aggressive and determined actions that are being called for here. They worry about betraying confidence and intruding into other people's private affairs, about being thought an alarmist and other similar concerns. These feelings arise in most concerned people, but they need to be balanced against the danger of an unnecessary and tragic death. When viewed from this perspective, those concerns seem strangely trivial. Clinical experience and research agree that when an individual has a well-thought-out suicidal plan, which is deadly, specific, and available, that person is highly likely to kill himself. The prevention of this death is worth the risk of transitory feelings of embarrassment or the breaking of a confidence which was ambivalently entered into in the first place.

If just one of Johnny's friends had taken the time to call his parents on that night and report to them what Johnny had reported to them three times, Johnny would be alive today, and in all probability, functioning successfully in some college, on his way to a creative and happy life. Had he been able to receive help and the support he was asking for, not only his own life but the lives of all those who were close to him would be substantially different. If Dr. Murphy's pastor had listened more carefully to his own feelings, as well as to the cloaked message that was being delivered to him by telephone on that fateful Saturday, if he had gone out on a limb to call Dr. Murphy's wife or daughter to share his concern and his fears, the life of a valuable physician might well have been extended.

Once a counselor has become aware of a carefully thought out suicide plan his first response should be to take the plan seriously, making certain that the suicidal victim himself is aware of the intensity of the danger. Suicidal people need to know that their message of desperation is getting through and is being heard and understood. Secondly, the counselor must be willing to involve himself for the moment, as the primary resource, the one link between life and death for this person at this time. Often this will call for an extended, intensive, interview encouraging the suicidal person to communicate the depth of his feelings of hopelessness and helplessness. The counselor should attempt to understand the severity of these feelings, and at the same time, do what he can to help discover other alternatives. Often as the result of such counselor involvement, the suicidal victim can be convinced to dispose voluntarily of the pills or unload the gun and give it to a friend, at least postponing his determination to die. If this can be accomplished, the counselor has not only purchased valuable time but has infused his client with the possibility of a different kind of resolution to his predictament. The immediate suicidal danger is now passed and again conscientious follow-through is the next demand.

A third level of intervention is appropriate when the situation is not as critical as in the first two levels. At level three, the suicidal victim has not yet developed a concrete suicidal plan, but is suffering from stress and is having difficulty mobilizing the resources he needs to deal with this stress. Any counselor can be of significant help in such situations if he helps the distressed person carefully evaluate the quality and nature of his personal resources, and helps him develop a plan for mobilizing them. Sometimes this will involve the counselor in making important telephone calls or, at times, in personal visits to people who have a concern for the suicidal person. At other times, once supported by his counselor, the suicidal person will be able to make these contacts himself. As a general rule, the patient ought to be permitted to do for himself whatever he can do, but if the counselor has doubts about his patient's ability to follow through with the plan of mobilizing resources, then he ought to involve himself more actively in such mobilization.

Frequently, callers to the Suicide Prevention Center of Los Angeles will report that they have a high number of personal resources, such as a husband or wife, parents, siblings, or friends, but for one reason or another they feel unable to reach out to these people. One such woman, Mrs. Duncan, called the center in the midst of an acute depression and was planning to kill herself. She reported that she has been married for two years and was very fond of her husband, but he was so busy trying to get established in his work that she felt that she had no right to be a burden to him and to confide in him her depressive and suicidal thoughts. Furthermore, she felt that his love for her depended on her not being depressed and suicidal. She feared that he would have no respect for her if he knew the desperate feelings that she was experiencing. After several interviews with a counselor at the center, she finally agreed to tell her husband that she had been seeking counseling and why. His response, although typical of many spouses in similar situations, was a complete surprise to her. He said that he had been aware for six months that she was depressed, that sometimes he would awaken in the middle of the night and hear her crying in the bathroom, but he was hesitant about intruding on her privacy thinking she didn't want to confide in him. Once the deadly secrecy was cut through with the help of the counselor, the suicidal danger dropped dramatically, and the couple involved themselves in marriage counseling, which helped provide a whole new basis for their marriage.

Frequently, teenagers will be so unhappy that they begin feeling suicidal, and they will tell their counselor that the last thing they want is for their parents to be informed. This is, of course, precisely the action that needs to be taken. Secrecy is always dangerous where suicide is concerned and the relief that comes once the secret no longer has to be kept usually provides immense new possibilities in the person's life.

Which resources need to be mobilized is a decision that can be made only on the basis of each individual patient. In Mrs. Lloyd's case, the key person was her husband. If the daughter had persisted in her perception of her mother as being seriously upset and had spoken to her family doctor or her clergyman, the appropriate action for this counselor would have been to talk directly to Mrs. Lloyd, and at the same time, to her husband, making clear to him the seriousness of the situation. His own resistance to acknowledging the truth would have to be handled with clinical sensitivity, but some way would have to be found to reach him.

Suicidal people characteristically suffer from strong feelings of isolation and alienation, and if they are not helped to make emotional contact with significant other people, the progress toward suicide will continue. If the counselor is alert and can recognize a developing suicidal situation at this level, he can forestall such development and, in many cases, terminate it permanently. The mobilizing of significant resources is the key and one of the best all around antidotes to suicidal behavior at any stage.

The fourth level involves supporting the individual's internal coping mechanisms. Many times, suicidal development can be abated early if the individual's own ego strength can be supported. Often, a reconstruction of the problem or a reconceptualization of the main issues is enough to stimulate the individual's own problem-solving abilities. Sometimes one can almost sense a mental block falling away and thrill at the flood of creative thinking and optimistic feeling that can surge forth to deal with what previously had been an unbearable stress. When one student, who for years had had his heart set on medical school, accepted the realization that he simply wasn't equipped for this lofty goal and was really much better suited to artistic endeavors, the relief with which he dropped the impossible internal demands was a pleasure to watch. A woman who had been having overwhelming feelings of guilt and shame and worthlessness because of certain secret sexual fantasies that she had been harboring for years, was being driven to serious thoughts of suicide until she was helped to see these fantasies as being a common experience of life to which she was bringing oppressive value judgments. Once she was able to mitigate this judgment, she was released from the suicidal demand. Another example is that of a twenty-one-year-old girl, who had been afflicted with Hodgkins disease since the age of twelve, and had been pampered by her protective mother since that time. She made three serious suicide attempts in response to her feelings of worthlessness and of being a terrible liability upon her family. When she was helped to see herself as a worthwhile person, who could contribute and perform meaningful work, the urge to suicide disappeared entirely and never returned, even when her disease gradually became worse and her physical powers lessened.

If a person has the basic ego strength to take responsibility for handling the stress or for seeking the support he needs, all a counselor may need to do is to help him mobilize his own internal strength and stand by him as he proceeds to find creative solutions to his own situation.

The fifth level of intervention into suicidal development has to do with alleviating early stressful situations. Especially with adolescents, the key to forestall suicidal behavior may be to remove oppressive stress once it has been identified. Often, this can be done by permitting the student to take a lighter load in school, or by working directly with the parents who may be making unrealistic demands for exceptional performance from an average youngster. This, according to Dr. Michael Peck of the Los Angeles center, is one of the leading causes for suicide among adolescents. If the stress of inappropriate parental demands can be alleviated most adolescents can respond in a creative way. Suicidal people often feel boxed in, locked into a situation which permits no resolution or solution. Often, this is an unrealistic internal demand which they place upon themselves. Sometimes, however, the structure of one's life should be changed when one needs the freedom to get out of a situation which is no longer satisfying or nurturing, but which continues to make incessant demands.

The sixth level of suicide prevention has been called, by Dr. Norman Farberow, "primary prevention." This takes place almost unconsciously in many areas of our culture where the question of suicide is not even recognized. Primary prevention consists of the maintenance of the normal social supports and services with which we surround our elderly and our ill. The withdrawal of these supports would almost surely result in a dramatic increase in the suicide rate. Probably the reverse is true—the expansion of such social services would result in a lowering of the suicide rate among this high risk population.

Suicide prevention and suicide crisis intervention takes place on many different levels and calls for different kinds of action, depending on how each individual situation presents itself and on how the suicidal potential is evaluated. This section has attempted to identify six specific levels of intervention and to detail some of the characteristics of each. One thing that is common to them all is the need for consistent follow-up.

Follow-Through

After his wife died, Mr. Gilbert experienced a severe and long-lasting depression, with terrible feelings of emptiness and purposelessness. Just six months prior to her death they celebrated their thirtieth wedding anniversary, looking back over the happy, secure years they had with each other. If there was any incompleteness in their marriage, it was that they had never had children, but they had never even thought seriously about adoption, evidently preferring the peacefulness of a close, childless marriage. It was just a few days after that happy anniversary that Mrs. Gilbert began complaining about some physical symptoms, and it was several weeks after that that her cancer was recognized and her physician had pronounced it inoperable giving her but a few months to live. Mr. Gilbert then resigned his job, wanting every possible moment at home with his wife. Although he was in line for substantial retirement benefits, his premature resignation terminated these benefits and left him with only a small savings.

He spent the next few months nursing Mrs. Gilbert, doing all that he could to keep her entertained, happy, and comfortable. She filled his life completely, and he had no interests outside of her welfare. When she died, therefore, he was left completely alone an feeling that he had no reason to continue living, although he was in good health and only fifty-seven years old. Having no family of his own, he lived temporarily with some distant relatives of his wife whom he liked, but with whom he had never been particularly close. These people received him graciously and said he could stay with them as long as he liked.

His depression began to increase with the passage of time, however, and it wasn't long before suicidal thoughts began to come into his mind, at first as a possible way of rejoining his beloved wife and later simply as a way of stilling the constant hurt and the ache of loneliness that was always with him. He began hoarding sleeping pills and playing with his rifle more and more. His in-laws observed some of this behavior, and becoming concerned they contacted a local suicide prevention center. He began seeing a counselor at the center, both in individual therapy and in supportive group work for several weeks. There was no noticable improvement. Instead, Mr. Gilbert continued feeling that he was imposing on his in-laws, and he began making plans to move out. He wanted to use some of the money that came from the sale of their house to buy a small trailer so that he could live out his years in a local trailer park where there were a number of elderly people, many of whom were alone. Although the plan seemed like an appropriate one to the counselor, he felt that it was premature and suggested that Mr. Gilbert postpone this plan, that he was probably not ready yet to move out on his own. His in-laws were making it clear that he was welcome to stay with them for a much longer time and, in fact, they were a little disappointed when he insisted on moving out.

It soon became apparent to the counselor that since Mr. Gilbert was not improving under short-term, crisis treatment and that a longer-term, deeper therapeutic experience was called for. The counselor suggested a reputable clinic in Mr. Gilbert's area and helped him make his first appointment. His reaction was lethargic and apathetic. He said that he didn't feel treatment would help him because there was no way to replace the loss of his wife. However, since he didn't have the energy to object, he would go along with the recommendations of the counselor, and he accepted the referral.

A month later it was discovered that Mr. Gilbert was dead. He had not gone beyond the first interview in the new mental health center, but had instead moved out from his in-law's house and rented a small trailer in the trailer park. It was on his third night alone in the trailer that he ingested a half a bottle of wine, an overdose of sleeping pills, and shot himself through the head with his rifle. His in-laws were badly shaken by what he had done, and for sometime afterward suffered severe guilt feelings for not having been able to prevent this death. The problem was that of inadequate follow-through. The crucial time was that of the transfer from one counselor and one clinic to another. This break in continuity left a time when no professional person felt that he had responsibility for Mr. Gilbert as a patient, and this was enough for this highly suicidal person to be overwhelmed again with the terrible feelings of abandonment and loneliness and to end his own life. The importance of consistent follow-through cannot be overstressed in the handling of highly suicidal people, and yet it is often lacking in many dangerous cases.

Mr. Hastings was found dead of a voluntary overdose of medication at the age of fifty-two. Investigation into the circumstances of this suicide revealed that he had taken a similar overdose and very nearly died six years earlier. At that time, he had written a suicide note and taken the overdose at a time when he felt he would be alone for a number of hours. He was fortuitously discovered by his wife and his life was barely saved. When Mrs. Hastings was asked what kind of follow-up there had been after this serious attempt, she replied that there was none. The hospital had simply pumped his stomach, cared for him medically while he was comatose for three days, and then released him when his physical health permitted. They made no psychiatric referral and no counseling was recommended. Mrs. Hastings also reported that she and her husband never talked about either the attempt or his reasons for it in the six years that followed. She knew nothing more about it than she did when it happened. It was simply never discussed. The result of this lack of follow-through was Mr. Hasting's death six years later.

Suicidal behavior can be understood as a manifestation of the patient's need for some basic change in his life. Medical treatment for a wound, just talking to someone about his feelings, or having someone understand his feelings of distress, are normally not enough for a suicidal individual, although these things may be a good and necesary start for the kind of change that is ultimately needed. What most seriously suicidal people need in addition to the opportunity to talk, and to be understood, is a basic change in their life circumstances. These changes often need to be major changes and may alter the whole course of their future lives. If things do not change, the chance of further suicidal behavior is very high.

The nature and quality of the actions that are taken after a suicidal hint, threat, or attempt, therefore, will often spell the difference between life and death, and yet many suicidal indications are not followed up by supposedly concerned people who are in touch with the distressed person. There are several possible reasons for failure in efficient follow-up. One may be a simple lack of resources within the life of the suicidal person. Many people who do not have adequate financial reserves, can find themselves in the position of having no one to turn to, of having no one who is sufficiently personally involved with them to take responsibility for their welfare during the duration of their suicidal crisis. The find themselves looking to public agencies which, although usually competent, cannot supply the personal involvement and caring that a seriously suicidal person needs. As in the case of Mr. Gilbert, the appropriate referral would be to an agency which can be of lifesaving help to him. But if the referral is to be successful, the patient may need to have someone accompany him to the new clinic for the first few appointments until rapport develops and he begins to feel he belongs. As mentioned above, the lack of such resources tends to increase the suicidal danger while, at the same time, it makes sufficient follow-up more difficult. Whoever works with such a person needs to be keenly aware of the seriousness of the situation.

Another common cause for the failure of follow-up in suicidal situations is to be found in the feelings of the significant other persons involved. Feelings of fatigue, for example, in someone who is seeking to help a seriously suicidal person, especially when the crisis has been going on for several days, may seriously hamper this person's ability to care and to provide the kind of continuing support that is necessary. Although the helper is doing all that he is able, he too has limitations, and when he begins to tire he may begin to lose interest and to wonder if all his efforts are really worth it. When such feelings of fatigue become pronounced they are frequently accompanied by conscious or unocnscious feelings of hostility toward the suicidal person. Such feelings, although they are a source of embarrassment sometimes to the helpers, are really logical and easily understood. "By what right," the helping person begins to feel, "does the person claim so much of my time, my energy, and my involvement? After all, the rest of us have to endure and survive by our own wits and our own internal strength, and I'm having a hard enough time in my life without having to carry the emotional burden of this person's distressed life too." Although such hostility extending sometimes to death wishes is understandable, if it is not consciously and carefully handled, it can have an important effect on the quality of follow-up support that one is able to give.

Another feeling on the part of the worker that can affect the quality of support is that of anxiety. Suicidal situations tend to produce a high anxiety level, and many people are uncomfortable being placed in the position of feeling responsible for another person's life. This anxiety and unsureness of their ability can often lead people to drop the "hot potato" and to pretend the situation does not exist. In the next section we will discuss the emotional problems of the would-be rescuer of suicidal people in more detail but perhaps it is already clear how such feelings can interfere with a sufficient follow-up procedure.

Another possible cause of inefficient follow-up is found in resistance offered by the patient. Many suicidal patients make their own rescue exceedingly difficult, attempting to thwart in every way they can the efforts of the helper. They can become provocative and stubborn, and can actually sabotage adequate follow-up plans. The reasons behind this kind of behavior lie in the flood of feelings that are issuing forth from the person who is in a suicidal crisis. He is often contradictory, inconsistent, and inappropriate in what he feels and how he acts and what he says. Wanting help desperately and yet fighting it at every turn is a common picture of many suicidal people. It is necessary for the helper to understand the extent to which this is happening and some of the reasons for it. If a patient is making it hard for himself to be helped then the worker needs to interpret this as an inability on the patient's part to participate in his own rehabilitation program, and decisions and plans need to be made for him by those who are able to carry them out in spite of this resistance.

A further reason that follow-up procedures are often not completed is that the crisis has not been accurately evaluated by the counselor and he has not realized that the distressed person is actually contemplating suicide. Perhaps this may stem from an inaccurate lethality evaluation.

Still another possible reason for incomplete follow-up procedure is that of ignorance on the part of the significant other people. As we have noted, many people are still laboring under the false assumption that people who talk about suicide do not actually do it. Some people are even comforted by the fact that a suicidal family member talks so much about suicide, seeing in this some kind of perverse reassurance that they are not actually planning to carry out what they are threatening.

Other kinds of helpers manifest their ignorance about the dynamics of suicide by taking inappropriate action. Some people believe it is helpful to suicidal people to provoke anger in them, and when they are confronted with suicidal communication they will become insulting, abusive, or challenging. The effect of this is negative for most suicidal people. They feel even more rejected and put down. It confirms their basic fear that they are unacceptable people and that they are not going to be helped. Such a response usually has the effect of pushing the suicidal person closer toward killing himself rather than the saving result that the helper may have intended.

Recommendations

The are many pitfalls and obstacles, therefore, standing in the way of adequate follow-up procedures. It is important that anyone dealing with a suicidal person be acutely aware of what the main issues and the dynamics of this person are, and what characteristics of an adequate follow-up will be. To be sufficient, the follow-up for a suicidal person should provide for at least four elements:

As was indicated in the last section, the first element should be sufficient, immediate support and coverage so that the suicidal person is not able to take his own life or to make a serious suicide attempt. This should include confiscation of the lethal means the suicidal person has selected, and constant attendance so that he is not left alone for the duration of the crisis. In most cases, this will mean that someone should be living with the patient, someone who is aware of the situation and who is concerned that the patient not take his own life. In some cases, it may be necessary that the patient be put in a protective environment, such as a hospital, where there is twenty-four hour, continuous protection for him. This total protection will probably be required only for the duration of the crisis, which can be only a few hours, and, at most, a few weeks. If effective follow-through procedures have been developed, these emergency procedures will soon become unnecessary.

The second necessary element in follow-up for suicidal people is the provision for substantial changes in his life situation. These changes should be responsive to the felt and expressed needs of the suicidal person and may necessitate other people changing some of their goals or living arrangements. Many suicidal adolescents, for example, who suffer from internalized demands that they become super students or high achievers may be driven to suicidal actions as a result of the impossibility of living up to these exalted expectations. It may be necessary in such families for parents to reevaluate carefully their expectations for their children and to make sure that these expectations are appropriate to their child's abilities and wishes. Usually professional help is needed for a family to readjust its unspoken and unconsciously assumed demands.

Sometimes a change in life-style, a change in occupation or occupational goals can have dramatic effect on alleviating suicidal feelings and plans. Dr. Murphy, for example, was feeling great pressure in his role as a physician. If someone could have helped him to systematically plan a way to shut down his private practice and move into some different area of his professional life, such as teaching, it might well have been that a whole new avenue would become open to him, and he could, once again, feel enthusiastic about living. Mrs. Richards was a school counselor who was feeling suicidal for several reasons, one of which was that she was feeling locked in and stifled in her profession. She felt that she needed the retirement benefits, and yet the work was becoming boring and confining to her. She was greatly relieved, and the suicidal thinking disappeared entirely when she began seriously considering the possibility of moving into other areas of work which were open to her. The result was that she made no actual change, but the confidence that she could do so permitted her to engage more freely and more creatively in work which had become, for her, deadly.

A third essential element in the follow-up planning for suicidal people is continuity. Mr. Gilbert died because there was none of this in his follow-up plans. He simply did not have the emotional strength to jump across the gap between two sources of help. If it is necessary for several people to be involved in the rehabilitation of a suicidal person, as indeed it normally is, great care must be taken that these various people coordinate with one another so that each is fully aware of the areas of responsibility of the other.

Continuity should also be maintained in terms of the kind of planning that is taking place. Contradictory plans, or chaotic courses of action, which do not move with one another have the result of confusing an already confused patient and making it appear that there is no way for his difficulty to be efficiently handled. The follow-up plan must, therefore, be carefully thought through by the significant people who are helping and changes from that plan made only after full discussion and coordination with all people involved.

A fourth characteristic of adequate follow-up is feasibility. Sometimes the things that suicidal patients ask for are simply impossible to deliver, they are just beyond the realm of reality. When this is the case, it must be carefully explained that what they want is impossible, but that other kinds of changes can be made and help is forthcoming to obtain them. It does little good to promise a suicidal patient something that is impossible to deliver because the failure only confirms in his mind the impossibility of being helped. In Mr. Gilbert's case, for example, it was simply impossible to provide him with what he wanted; that is, his wife alive and well again. However, it should have been possible to create some kind of plan to provide him with support and security and which, in time, would offer him the opportunity to become emotionally involved once again in a satisfying way with people to whom he could relate intimately. It may be impossible to provide a passing grade or a diploma to a failing suicidal youngster, and any plan which attempts this is probably unfeasible. What can be done, however, is to help the student understand why he is failing and to help him make whatever adjustments are called for to enable him to cope more adequately with the demands that he faces. A plan for the prevention of a suicide must be realistic in terms of what can be accomplished.

Counselor Response

Overreaction

Marsha, a seventeen-year-old junior high student, was rushed, tears streaming down her face and holding her left arm which was soaked in her own blood, into the school nurse's office by her physical education teacher.

"She was trying to kill herself," reported the teacher. "I found her just in time in the locker room with a razor blade, cutting her wrists."

Mrs. Davis, a school nurse for over twenty years, became frightened, reached for the telephone and called the suicide prevention center. When the counselor came on the line, Mrs. Davis fairly shouted in the telephone, "There's a student in my office who's made a suicide attempt, and who's bleeding badly from her left arm. What shall I do?"

The counselor asked, "Have you stopped the bleeding yet?"

"No."

"I suggest you stop the bleeding, see how serious the wound is, provide medical treatment, and then call me back."

Such advice seems simplistic and unnecessary when related weeks after the actual event, but at the time of the crisis even experienced professional people are susceptible to feelings of panic and intense anxiety, and can omit nor-

127

mal, helpful courses of action which they are trained and competent to perform. The nurse had become so overwhelmed at the mention of suicide that she abandoned her own professional role. If the same wound had been inflicted under other circumstances, an accident on the playground, for example, the nurse would have been able to function in her normal, professional, and competent way. It was the word "suicide" that produced the panic and the inappropriate action.

Mrs. Davis' experience is not unusual. Many people who can respond to dangerous crisis situations with appropriate presence of mind become upset and inefficient when the threat of suicide is imminent. So emotionally laden is the word and the act, that many professional psychotherapists, who routinely deal with all sorts of other kinds of unpleasant behavior, refuse to accept suicidal patients. Most clergymen, however, do not have the luxury of deciding whether to accept or not accept suicidal parishioners. Their task is to tend the flock and to be responsive to whatever needs arise within that context. They must, therefore, learn to deal creatively with the unpleasant feelings that are produced by suicidal threats and attempts.

As anyone who has worked with people knows, feelings are contagious. It is impossible to work with a depressed person and not experience feelings of depression. One cannot try to understand the emotions of a confused person without becoming confused. This is especially true if a patient is in a state of emotional crisis where the feelings are more intense. When depression turns to despair and confusion to chaos, the counselor is automatically involved in the deep and intense feelings.

A crisis involves the emotions of the counselor in a second

way through the response that he is called upon to make. In most noncrisis counseling situations the counselor is on familiar ground. The interview usually takes place in his own office, and he knows by his training and years of experience what is expected of him. He is to remain empathic, supportive, sometimes interpretative, and relatively passive. Initiative is to be taken only by the patient and, in most cases, the counselor is enjoined by training and by ethics against taking much initiative action on his own. In a crisis situation, however, just the reverse may be true. Unable to make appropriate decisions or take appropriate actions on his own behalf, the patient often looks to his counselor to assume the responsibility and the activity that he can no longer provide for himself. This places the counselor in a whole new role which inevitably arouses anxiety. He is now in command and must make the kinds of decisions which will preserve the life of the suicidal patient while respecting the feelings and the integrity of other people. He is, in short, in a whole new relationship in which the guidelines and boundaries are ill defined and in which the outcome may be seriously in question and vitally important. It is no wonder that many people want to avoid being placed in such a situation where there are so many difficult feelings to handle and so few rules to protect them.

So far many of the feelings that the counselor is subject to have been mentioned. The feelings of panic that were experienced by Mrs. Davis, feelings of anger and resentment toward an over-demanding suicidal patient, feelings of fatigue when the crisis drags on into days and weeks, feelings of fear that the situation may at any time break out of control, feelings of frustration and inferiority when nothing seems to work, all are common and inevitable on the part of someone seeking to prevent the suicide. If these feelings are inevitable, the importance of understanding and handling them is a necessity. To overreact to a suicidal patient, to panic and be overwhelmed by feelings of anxiety, usually results in the stimulation of even more chaos and confusion. This predictably has the effect of preventing help or at least making aid more difficult. A school counselor, for example, heard one of his student's expressing suicidal thoughts. He immediately began telephoning the boy's parents, physician, and clergyman to apprise them of the immediate danger of the situation. When the boy—who was not seriously suicidal—learned of this, he was hurt and angry at the overreaction and at the breach of confidence. In this situation the feelings of the child were ignored and the feelings of the counselor took over center stage and dictated the action and the course of the relationship. Any child is apt to come away from such an encounter feeling that he has been misunderstood and that appropriately responsive help is not going to be available to him.

It isn't only suicide, of course, which tends to produce violent overreaction on the parts of significant other people. Some parents tend, for example, to overreact to the discovery that their high school child has been smoking marijuana and some have even been known to call in the police to correct a situation which was really nothing more serious than a curious youngster experimenting in a mild way with something with which his culture has become fascinated.

Underreaction

Some clergymen and counselors handle difficult feelings in the opposite way. They become so conscious of the negative influence of overreaction that they flee to the other end of the continuum and respond to a serious crisis by under-reacting. These are the "super cool" counselors who take great pride in being worldly-wise and unshockable. They rest in their own emotional fortress flying the flag, secure that nothing can shake them and nothing can excite them. Such denial of feeling usually comes across to the upset suicidal person as a withholding. Such counselors are usually interpreted as being unresponsive and uncaring and certainly inappropriate. The fact is, that suicidal situations *are* threatening; they are dangerous and they should stimulate responsive feelings. By denying these feelings in an effort to remain cool and unshaken the counselor runs the danger of becoming immobilized and unable to respond in an appropriate way to a life and death emergency.

Inappropriate Action

A third way which a counselor may mishandle his feelings in the midst of a crisis is by taking inappropriate action which simply misses the point. Henry S., a twenty-year-old philosophy major, had made three suicide attempts within a year. Although a very bright, capable person, who had come through high school and the first couple of years of college with straight *A*'s, his grades, in the last year, were down to *C*'s and he was now in danger of failing two courses. He had made extensive experimentation with most drugs and was on a moderate high most of the time. When his school counselor attempted to discuss with him the seriousness of his situation, he found himself continually being seduced into a philosophical discussion on the moral and philosophical right of a person to kill himself, or perhaps the social implications of the legalization of marijuana.

These discussions, which would go on at some length, were interesting to both participants but they simply missed the point—that here was a boy who was emotionally out of control and who was on the brink of killing himself. These discussions on the philosophic and ethical moral rights of an individual in a general sense were totally irrelevant to Henry's feelings and emotions. The discussions represented a conspiracy of avoidance which permitted both the patient and the counselor to be shielded from the intense feelings of fear and despair that the patient was experiencing and which were leading him to multiple suicide attempts. Fortunately, in this case, the student was referred to a therapist who would not permit such deflection and who insisted on focusing on feelings specifically and personally so that they could be dealt with. Once the student saw that this counselor was not frightened of dealing directly with these feelings, he felt more capable of doing this, too, and the crisis was soon resolved.

Guiding Principles

There are several principles which are applicable to all crisis work and which have special relevance to the counselor who will be working with suicidal people.

The first principle is the necessity for the counselor to evaluate his own feelings and not to permit denial, repression, deflection, or panic to take place. The counselor needs access to his feelings in order to be sensitive to the emotional data before him. Although much information about the suicidal person can come to the counselor in the form of facts and verbal descriptions, some of the most important material that he will need comes to him through the alertness of his own feelings and the ability to remain sensitive to the nonspoken clues that his patient is communicating. He needs the ability to listen to both the words and the music if he is genuinely to understand his patient emotionally. When the counselor's own feelings are too intense or when he is so afraid of them that he either deadens them or permits them to take stage center, he has sacrificed one of his most important assets. The counselor needs the ability to feel fear when he is afraid, to feel upset when he is anxious, to feel sexual feelings when he is being aroused, to feel anger and hate when he is being provoked, to feel resentment when the is being put down, to feel manipulated when a manipulation is taking place. When he sacrifices this ability he has sacrificed his appropriateness and his capacity for a fitting response to his patient.

Once his feelings are acknowledged the effective counselor next needs to identify them so that he is not simply experiencing them on some preconscious or unconscious level. He must be able to label them and to describe them to himself. The ability and the discipline of accomplishing this provides the counselor with objectivity and insures that he will not be engulfed by his feelings, but will be able to make appropriate decisions on the basis of them.

Once the feelings have been consciously experienced and identified, the counselor will want to evaluate the feelings in terms of their appropriateness and their source. Some of the feelings that arise will appear to be out of context with the rest of the interaction. Although consciously believing everything that the patient is telling him, the counselor may be aware that a side of him is remaining very skeptical and unresponsive. He will want to evaluate these feelings and test them. Is he picking up another side to the patient that he had not been previously aware of, or is the counselor himself acting defensively, not wanting to believe what seems to him to be a frightening and uncontrollable situation? Although feeling sympathetic and warm toward the patient, he may, at the same time, be aware of some feelings of anger and hostility. Is he resentful because he is being inconvenienced or, on the other hand, do the feelings arise in response to some quality in the patient, and are they related to the fact that he suffers periodic rejection from people close to him?

Many times, in dealing with suicidal people, the counselor will be aware that the effect being communicated does not fit with the words being spoken. For example, the patient may be relating a terrible life history that includes severe losses and experiences of brutality, but relating these horror stories in a calm, smiling way. At other times, the reverse may be true. The incidences which the patient is relating may seem to the counselor to be rather trivial and common, and yet the patient will be reacting with violent and intense feelings that are out of proportion to the stress that he is revealing. When the counselor observes such phenomena he must take them seriously and search out the explanation for the apparent contradiction.

Whenever one is dealing with a patient in crisis, especially if that crisis includes the possibility of suicide, he should always have competent consultation available. No counselor should be expected to deal with suicidal persons in isolation. The possibility of suicide produces too much anxiety and places too much responsibility on the shoulders of one person. Consultation can provide several advantages. First, it can help the counselor identify and evaluate his own feelings, keeping them in a workable perspective and helping him maintain his own emotional balance. A second benefit of consultation is the opportunity to test out the appropriateness of possible plans of action, to stimulate the development of other alternatives, and to explore the possibility of overlooked opportunities. Finally, the consultant may have other sources of information in regard to community resources that may not have come up in the original conversations with the suicidal person.

Although consultation should make use of professional people who have special training in the field, sometimes they are not easily available. Good consultation can often be provided by the counselor's own peer group, concerned and mature men and women who, while not having more training than the original counselor, nevertheless, can serve a valuable function as a sounding board and supportive friend.

Each counselor can find his own way to handle the intense feelings that arise in situations where suicide is a possibility. The important thing is that he make a conscious effort to recognize and evaluate his own feelings honestly, and use this knowledge for the benefit of his patient.

Chapter 4
The Aftermath of Suicide

The shot that broke the silence on that quiet Sunday afternoon made her freeze. The silence following that terrible noise was even more ominous than the shot itself had been, and she slowly made her way back up the hallway into the den where she had just left her husband cleaning his rifle. The sight that confronted her was sickening. Blood was everywhere, and crumpled on the floor of the den, with the top of his head missing, lay the body of her husband.

Her memory of the events following is jumbled and unclear. There was the telephone call, the police, the confusion, the concern about their thirteen-year-old daughter, contacting their married son, the doctor, the men from the coroner's office, the funeral director, the minister, friends, relatives, the questions, the confusion. How did it happen? And then the word that had been avoided all along: suicide. "They think he committed suicide. They say he killed himself deliberately; that he wanted to die."

It took several days for that thought to come to the surface of Mrs. King's mind. The shock, the confusion, the thousand questions and details and feelings that normally attend the sudden death of someone close, began to recede and in her mind only one question of any importance remained. Could it be that he really did take his own life? Could he really have left her so finally and so deliberately? Why? Why would he do that? Her mind went back over twenty-five years of marriage searching for a clue. They had faced many hard times together. Their first son had been born with a heart defect that meant his premature death at the age of twenty. Then followed the long war years from 1942-45 which had meant separation for the young family. But after the war there was the arrival of a second son, followed by the birth of a daughter eleven years later. These were happy years. Mrs. King was happy in her Methodist Church, singing in the choir, teaching Sunday school and working in the woman's society. Mr. King never attended but she had reconciled to that, and he had never objected to the children's involvement.

Then five years ago he suffered a back injury that forced him to give up the only work he really knew how to do. He was idle for a year recuperating, and then he found a boring routine job that he had held since. She had known that he was unhappy with his work. He had never talked much about it. She was half aware that his drinking was increasing, that he was depressed, and that he was having trouble sexually for the first time in his life.

"But suicide? How could that be? It just couldn't, that was all," she assured herself. "It just couldn't have happened that way. It was an accident. It must be certified an accident.

"But how did the gun happen to be loaded? Why would he load the gun? How did it come to be pointed at his head? Accidental. It was accidental. The gun was loaded because there had been prowlers. That was it. About a year ago, the house had been broken in to. He had probably loaded the gun and then forgotten. And then when he was cleaning it, it just went off. It must have been an accident.

"Maybe he heard rumors about me. Maybe he heard bad things about me. Maybe he believed them."

Mrs. King had recently taken a job with the local school district.

"Maybe he heard I talked to the father of that little black boy. Maybe someone at work made up stories about me and him. Maybe that's why he hasn't come to me lately. Maybe he thinks I've been doing bad things. Maybe that's why he killed himself."

It was suggested to Mrs. King that she receive help during this complicated and difficult time of mourning. She did consult her family doctor who talked to her for awhile, prescribed some medication, and suggested that she receive more extensive counseling; but her thinking was becoming so obsessed by suspicions that she found reasons why she should not do this. Private treatment was eliminated because she couldn't afford it, and a public agency that might have been of some help, she eliminated because "they keep records and anything I say might be reported to the school district and I might lose my job."

It was next suggested that she talk with her pastor.

"I could never do that. You know, he has been avoiding me ever since the funeral. He even seems strange when we shake hands on Sunday mornings after church. It's like he doesn't want to talk to me, doesn't want to get close to me. After all the time I've given that church. Others in the congregation, too, they avoid me. Supposedly good friends who came to call for awhile after the funeral, they never call now. They even avoid speaking to me when they do see me. Do you know what I think? I think they talk about me. They think it's my fault. They're even spreading rumors about me."

Mrs. King became more suspicious and accusatory as time went on. She became convinced that people were against her and she withdrew increasingly into her own unhappy world of isolation, depression, and suspicion.

Normal Grief Reactions

The process of normal grief has been the subject of much study and observation in recent years. Lindemann, for example, found five basic aspects in the normal grief response.

1. The person who is suffering grief will often experience somatic disturbances. Physical symptoms, such as shortness of breath, sweating, indigestion, some difficulty in talking, are common.

2. Preoccupation with the image of the loss person is another important characteristic of a normal grief reaction. The person has difficulty in getting his mind off his own loss and experiences severe difficulty in entertaining new subjects and concentrating on new issues.

3. Strong feelings of guilt are usually observable in the normal grief reaction. Often these feelings are inappropriate and somewhat vague. The survivor will feel that he ought to have done more even when any objective evaluation of his activities would reveal that he literally did everything that could have been done. Often, the person's mind will reach back into prior years and recount in an obsessional

way all the sins of commission and omission that were perpetrated against the deceased.

4. Feelings of hostility and anger toward the deceased become apparent. The survivor is feeling abandoned and resents having to face life alone without the accompaniment of one he depended on.

5. The loss of regular behavior patterns, including the loss of energy to perform usual tasks is experienced by the survivor. He often has the experience that something is holding him back from engaging in what had been normal activities.[1]

Westberg has developed ten stages which represent the regular progression of grief which most individuals experience.

1. At first, the person is stunned when he hears the news of the death. The effect is to be anesthetized against the impact of the loss. He often verbalizes this first denial, even when he is beginning to accept, with such phrases as, "Oh, no!" or, "It can't be." Sometimes the anesthetization is so strong that the person faints and looses consciousness.

2. Once the initial stunned stage is passed, emotions begin to come forth, and the person experiences them, at first, in a diffuse and vague way, feeling intensely upset. He may weep copiously or experience other kinds of physical and emotional symptoms.

3. Depression is the third stage in which a person begins to experience the object lost, and he feels empty and blue.

4. The fourth stage is marked by physical disturbances which may take the form of physical illness, loss of energy, aches and pains, or the reoccurrence of previously experi-

---

[1] Erich Lindemann, "Symptomotology and Management of Acute Grief," *Pastoral Psychology,* 14 (September, 1963), 8-18.

enced disease. Sometimes the person will experience some symptoms that the deceased was experiencing prior to his demise.

5. Feelings of panic, not knowing what to do next, fear of what may become of him, along with doubts about one's ability to cope or make appropriate decisions follow.

6. Guilt feelings, as described above, are another important stage.

7. Hostility is often experienced, taking the form of resentment toward the deceased for no longer being there to account for his actions and to help the bereaved deal with his intense feelings.

8. The person may find himself unable to adopt the normal attitudes of life. He may feel especially picked on or unfairly treated by life or he may feel himself special in some way.

9. Hope begins to dawn as the person moves through the progression of these stages, and he begins to have the feeling that he is, indeed, going to be able to survive and to adjust to the loss and to make a new life for himself.

10. Stage number ten is characterized by a readjustment to the new reality of the person's life.[2]

Jackson, another well-known student of grief reaction, specifies the psychological process of identification with the lost person, substitution of other objects for the lost person, and guilt feelings, as being the most important phases of grief and those in which people are most likely to have difficulty.[3]

---

[2] Granger Westberg, *Good Grief* (Philadelphia: Fortress Press, 1962).
[3] Edgar Jackson, *Understanding Grief* (Nashville: Abingdon Press, 1957).

Grief Reactions Following a Suicide

The Surviving Spouse

In the case of suicidal deaths, the normal grief process is intensified and more difficult at every stage. Not every survivor of a suicide reacts with the intensity of Mrs. King, but the emotional and social issues that she faced are typical of anyone suffering a personal loss through suicide.

The beginning trauma of a suicidal death is usually significantly more severe than in most other deaths. In the case of most natural deaths the survivors have had the opportunity to begin to work through some of their feelings prior to the death itself. They often have been informed by their physician and by their own observation that death is coming, and though they may experience a stunned reaction when the final moment has arrived, the impact is far less than when death comes in a totally unexpected way, as is the case with most suicides. Mrs. King had not been consciously aware of her husband's plan to kill himself. Hearing the shot and discovering the grotesque body is an experience which would be deeply upsetting to anyone. The fact that, on another level, Mrs. King had been dimly aware of her husband's depression and mounting dissatisfaction with his job and himself, only intensified her need not to face these emotional issues directly and made the final traumatic breakthrough of reality even more difficult to handle.

When the preliminary shock began to lift and her emotions started coming, she faced further difficulty. Society prescribes certain ways in which grief should procede and in which emotions are to be expressed and handled when the death is normal and natural. What one "should" be feeling, what feelings are acceptable and appropriate in the case of a suicide, however, is far less clear, and the grieving person is left without the same kind of socially defined structure as to what feelings to have and how to express them. In addition, terrible questions of how or why often have to be filled in with speculation and imagination. Death by suicide carries with it its own special burden of shame and guilt for the survivor.

The depression following the suicide can be so intense that the survivor feels there is no way for him to handle it, and he may become suicidal himself. Physical disturbance may become more complicated and intensified and the feeling of panic, of not knowing what to do next or how others are going to respond to the tragedy can be of major significance.

Although all these grief reactions are intensified as a result of a suicide, the major problem lies in the area of the survivor's feelings of guilt. In many cases, as was the case with the King family, the relationship between the spouses in the years leading to the suicide event was not very close or untroubled, although Mrs. King worked hard at maintaining the pretense. At least from the time of his back injury five years prior to his death, Mr. King had been having trouble with depression and had sought to handle growing feelings of despondency and impotency by withdrawal and by increased drinking. She responded to the growing disturbance in her husband mainly by denial and avoidance. She had a deep-seated need to pretend and to act as if things were good, and she continually looked toward the externals of their life as evidence that life was going smoothly for both of them. She was convinced that her husband was reasonably happy because he "ought to have been happy." He had every reason to be proud of his son, who was married; his daughter, who was growing up well; and of their growing financial security. She, herself, was too threatened to recognize that, in fact, her husband was very unhappy and depressed and was getting worse. The result was that the Kings were growing more and more out of touch with one another and were losing the intimacy that had characterized their marriage in years previous. Now, with the blatant fact of his suicide, Mrs. King was having all the more difficulty with feelings of guilt, knowing that somehow she had missed the desperately unhappy feelings of her husband.

If one normally feels guilty over the natural death of someone close, it's easy to understand how these feelings of guilt are intensified in the case of a suicidal death. The feeling that if one had only known he might have been able to prevent it, are usually strong.

At the same time that strong feelings of guilt are being experienced, feelings of hostility and resentment are also rising in the survivor's mind. Many suicides can be understood as an attack on someone close. In some cases, it is a dramatic way of having the last word and leaving the survivor with strong feelings of frustration and anger, which are difficult to discharge and to handle. The anger and guilt tend to play upon one another, making it difficult to work through either. How can one be openly angry at a deceased person when one carries such a guilt about the death, and how resolve the guilt feelings when he is so angry?

Still another difficulty that the survivor of a suicidal death experiences is the loss of the usual social support that most grieving people heavily rely upon. Mrs. King experienced a certain estrangement from her pastor and from friends and members of her church congregation. Part of this was, no doubt, due to her own feelings of guilt and shame which made it difficult for her to be close to people. But partly it was the result of the feelings that most people have when a suicidal death occurs. Even in an age as enlightened as our own, the stigma and the superstition about suicide remains strong. People who respond well and warmly in other kinds of tragedies feel embarrassed and put off when a suicidal death has occurred. They become frightened and anxious and frequently respond by withholding support and avoiding the primary survivors. The result of this, of course, is that the grieving person feels ostracized and his feelings of abandonment and aloneness are intensified. He often reads this as being confirmation of his guilt feelings and the process of grief becomes even more difficult.

Being unable to accept the reality of a suicidal death is one main characteristic of failure to work through a normal grief reaction. If the person feels that he cannot afford the emotional reality of suicide, he will often simply deny the suicide has taken place, but then he is left with the problem of explaining to himself what really did happen. Strange, and often bizarre, hypotheses commonly come to mind as attempts to explain the tragedy of such a death. The myth of a mysterious prowler is one of the most common fantasies employed by people seeking to avoid a direct confrontation with suicide. They will convince themselves and attempt to convince other people, that an unknown intruder entered and committed homicide. If a person is emotionally committed to this explanation, even the most thoroughgoing police investigation will be of no avail, and the person will frequently persevere in the suspicion and sometimes feel that his life is in jeopardy. In other cases, the survivor will take it upon himself to conduct an elaborate investigation into circumstances surrounding the suicidal death of a loved one. In one case, a brother of a deceased girl became convinced that the suicidal death was homicide and that she had been killed by her husband. The brother took it upon himself to amass a huge amount of material, covering every facet of the deceased's life, seeking to prove that she could not have killed herself. He continued searching out every secret of her husband's life, involving present and past employers, the police department, the coroner's office, and the district attorney's office to find support for his dedicated belief that his sister was the victim, not of a suicidal depression, but of an evil, cunning bluebeard.

Sometimes this suspicion and confusion center in on the survivor himself as was the case with Mrs. King. She began to imagine that people were plotting against her and that she was being victimized by malicious rumors of sexual misconduct. If her husband's suicide could be blamed on some terrible misunderstanding, or if the blame could be laid at the feet of "them," those who had been carrying untrue and malicious rumors about her, her guilt could finally be put to rest.

The problem with all these rationalizations, fanciful intruders and other hypotheses, is that they are attempts to repress the truth and avoid dealing with the relevant emotional issues and so are never satisfying. The survivor is thus damned to pursue illusion and may well dedicate years of his life following these will-o'-the-wisps.

The Surviving Child

The surviving children of a suicidal parent have special problems in coping with the tragedy. The actual event of the suicide usually produces the same intense feelings of shock, guilt, and anger that a surviving adult faces. The child, too, usually suffers with problems of social stigma and threatened ostracization, which are often even more difficult for him because of his immature ego structure.

In addition to these troubles with the suicide itself, the child usually has had a troubled relationship with the parent. Some young children have been known to make relationship is marked by a lack of intimacy and concern that usually accompanies depression or severe preoccupation. The child may already have serious doubts about his value in his parent's eyes, and therefore about his intrinsic worth as a human being. This problem is, of course, intensified after the suicidal death, for this leaves the child a half-orphan, and deprives him entirely of exposure to one parent. Some young children have been known to make suicide attempts in the belief that they would join the absent parent in death or "with God," thereby correcting the loss. This is true not only of children whose parents have killed themselves, but also those who have suffered the loss of a parent either through natural or accidental death or through some extended absence, as in the case of a father serving an extended military hitch.

Another effect on the child is that he tends to learn that suicide is a possible way of handling stress. Children learn from their parents, using them as models and adopting various forms of behavior throughh imitation. In later years, when difficult times arise, the idea of suicide is already there as an alternative and an internalized suggestion.

There is little direct research in the literature on the subject of the effects of suicidal deaths upon the surviving children. T. L. Dorpat, M.D., has made certain observations of the long-term psychological effects of parental suicide on surviving children. He finds that the presuicide trauma, including severe marital discord, parental psychosis, and parental suicide attempts, were significant contributors to later disturbance. The postsuicide trauma, including the loss of at least one, and sometimes both parents, and the failure of surviving relatives to provide sufficient support for the child's ego strain were major factors. In addition, strong feelings of guilt frequently led to self-destructive behavior, depression and some arrest of their psycho-sexual developments. In addition to the guilt, Dorpat sees rage over the rejection and abandonment by the parent to have significant negative effects. Both the shock trauma of the suicide and the more prolonged state of ego strain combined to make healthy adjustment difficult.[4]

The Surviving Parent

To accept the fact that one's child has killed himself is simply beyond the ability of most parents. Psychological defenses are usually needed to soften the abrupt encroachment of a terrible reality which, as we have seen in other relationships, raises strong feelings of guilt, anger, and a pervading sense of failure and bewilderment. The parental reaction to adolescent suicide can take many different forms from that of simple denial of the suicide, while accepting the fact of death, to denial of the suicide accompanied by severe agitation and depression, to detachment and repression, to an aggressive, angry denial of the fact, to acceptance of the suicidal death while placing the blame on some outside influences.

---

[4] Theodore Dorpat, "Psychological Effects of Parental Suicide on Surviving Children" (manuscript).

The most common example of the latter is the reaction of one man to the suicide of his nineteen-year-old daughter, who leaped from a tall building to her death. Although there was no question of the death's being a suicide the focus of attention for this man and his family was on his daughter's use of drugs in the years preceding her death. He considered her a victim of the drug culture and dedicated much time and money to the drug programs of his community. The trauma of a daughter dead by suicide was muted for him as he was able to place blame on the "enemy," drugs, and then proceed to take specific action to fight the enemy in his daughter's behalf. This reaction was certainly more constructive than the reaction of another man who felt that his daughter, who died by an overdose of drugs, was driven to her death by the crowd she was hanging around with, specifically one young man. Having thus identified the enemy he set out on his plan of vengeance by conducting a widescale investigation into this young man's life and plaguing him for years afterward, interfering in opportunities for employment and even schooling. Both fathers were manifesting an emotional need to find an external cause for their daughters' suicidal deaths and each sought to handle his own grief by attacking the supposed cause, to even the score. The social consequences of the way each man went about this were, of course, quite different.

Another way in which parents frequently handle the suicide of a child has been mentioned earlier. Parents of Suzie H. returned home one evening to find their daughter dead of an overdose of barbiturates. Unable, emotionally, to accept the fact of suicide, they accepted the myth of a mysterious intruder, whom they decided entered the home and forced the pills down their daughter's throat, causing her death. Having then decided that it was death by homicide, they went about the process of collecting clues. Although the case was carefully investigated by the police department, the parents demanded a reinvestigation and an examination of the first set of investigating officers. When this second inquiry was completed with the same results, instead of being able to accept this, it simply reinforced their own defenses. They became more convinced than ever that not only was the death of their daughter a homicidal death but that somehow someone had gotten to the police department. These angry, articulate people became so aggressive that they even received time on the local radio station interview show where they began calling for reform for the local police department. Another investigation by the district attorney's office simply indicated, once again, that the death was a suicide and the case was finally dropped, but only after considerable expense and unfair accusations against the police. These parents are still unconvinced that their daughter could have killed herself and after several years are still extremely agitated and tense, being unable to either accept or to let go of the tragedy which has befallen them.

The family of Jimmy R. represents still another pattern of parental adjustment to adolescent suicide. Jimmy killed himself with an overdose of barbiturates in an act which was completely unpredicted by his family. Jimmy's mother reacted by becoming physically ill and confined to her bed for the next nine months. She had a variety of physical symptoms, including severe headaches and nausea, general weakness, loss of appetite, and an overall inability to function. Although never physically strong, the death of her son seemed to be the last straw for her, and she retreated into the world of hypochrondria. Jimmy's father, a salesman, found himself totally unable to work for four months following his son's death. He became irritable and angry, and his thought processes became jumbled and inconsistent. He demanded an investigation of his son's death, convinced that it could not have been a suicide. When the investigating officer called, however, he refused to cooperate with the investigation and would give no information. He simply asserted that it was impossible that his son had killed himself and the investigating officer should agree with him. When pressed for more information about his son's background and current stress, the father would respond in an agitated and confused way. He became gradually more and more isolated as the terrible conflict within was repressed.

Still another way in which some parents handle the fact of a suicidal death of their child is by detachment and repression. The parents of an eighteen-year-old Marine, who shot himself while home on leave for Christmas vacation, simply withdrew from having anything to do with the funeral and the burial. It was as if their son never belonged to them, and they simply refused to take any responsibility for the event. The only request that they made of anyone was that their other children not be told that the death was by suicide. They had told them that it was an accident and that was that. The funeral arrangements were handled by friends, and although the parents attended the funeral, they never betrayed any sign of emotion or involvement, and returned to their lives as if nothing had happened. Such a reaction is not as rare as one might think and leaves one to speculate how total the rejection and detachment must have been for years prior to the tragic death.

Still another way that parents have been observed handling their reaction to suicide of a child was that of Mr. and Mrs. George. Their nineteen-year-old son killed himself with an overdose of medication, but only after eighteen months of intense pain, suffering, and hospitalization due to cancer which everyone knew was terminal. After telling several people that the pain was too much to bear any longer, he took an overdose of the medication which the nurse had left in the room by accident. The parents never admitted, either to themselves or others, that it was a suicidal death. They called it accidental and seemed very much at peace with the event. It is not surprising that the mourning process of these parents should be much easier than that of the others described here. What may be surprising, however, is the fact that even under these extreme circumstances the parents found it necessary to deny the fact of the suicide. Even when a strong case could be made for the rationality and the moral acceptability for the act, still the stigma, as far as these parents are concerned, was too high a price to pay and they relied on the defense of denial.

As we have observed in the cases of the surviving spouse and the surviving child, the manner in which surviving parents handle their grief at the loss of a suicided child is complicated by the fact there usually has been a troubled relationship between them for years prior to the death. In some of the cases mentioned in this section, there had been a background of overt violence and undisguised hatred between at least one parent and the child. In the last case mentioned, that of the nineteen-year-old with terminal cancer, the wish that the boy would die had been nearly conscious, yet never quite acceptable to his parents. When the wish comes true, when the child by his own volition invites his own death in obedience to unrealized parental commands, the effects on the emotions of the parents, is often monumental. One is in the position then of having either to take responsibility for one's own unconscious death wishes toward another, or to repress them even deeper even to the point of denying that the event took place. This, then, is the issue which the parent must decide and it is not surprising that most often the result is denial and repression—not of the death but of the essential quality of that death—which is the willfulness of it.

There has been little formal research conducted in the area of parental response to adolescent and child suicides. One such study, however, was conducted by Herzog and Resnick. Their findings support the clinical observations just reported.

The researchers investigated nine adolescent suicides which occurred in Philadelphia during 1965 and 1966. No address could be found for the parents of two of the suicides, but the parents of the remaining seven were studied. The adolescents were between the ages of twelve and eighteen. The parents were contacted between two months and two years after the death. Of the seven families investigated, one did not respond at all to the request for an interview, three filled out a questionnaire but would not consent to an interview, and three sets of parents consented to both.

One of the striking findings that the researchers discovered was the frequency of family disruption. At the time of the child's suicide, nearly half of the parents were either divorced, separated, or married for the second time, and the adolescents were out of contact with one parent.

Investigators further found that the immediate parental

response to the sudden loss of their adolescent by suicide appeared to be "overwhelming hostility and denial followed by guilt and depression." These parents normally expressed their anger toward other people tangently involved in the death, such as policemen, hospital attendants, or physicians. The investigators observed that "this defense allows them to immediately, albeit it temporarily, externalize the stress. The more they project their guilt the less they face it within themselves." [5]

The investigators also found that all the parents interviewed expressed some form of denial. "The denial of the death as a suicide appeared an effort by the parents to extricate themselves from what they call a 'dishonor' suicide brings upon their name. On a deeper, dynamic level, they deny their involvement, sometimes real, sometimes imagined, in the suicide. These parents simply maintain that the death was an accident or a murder. . . ." [6] The investigators also felt that they were in very real danger of breaking down very fragile defenses that the parents had erected, defenses which they needed, so the investigators did not pursue evidence that the death was, in fact, a suicide.

Another finding was that the parents of adolescent suicides "were quite emphatic about not wanting another child. Although they tried, none could hide their guilt. It seemed as though . . . they were constantly saying to them-

[5] Alfred Herzog and H. L. P. Resnik, "A Clinical Study of Parental Response to Adolescent Death by Suicide with Recommendations for Approaching the Survivors," *Proceedings of the Fourth International Conference for Suicide Prevention* (ed. Norman L. Farberow), Los Angeles, 1967, p. 381.
[6] *Ibid.,* p. 384.

selves, "we have failed with one child. We don't wany anyone to blame us for failing with another."

Social isolation, withdrawal, self-accusation, insomnia and
sadness pervaded the interviews. These feelings are strongest
the closer the interview was to the time of death, but were
clearly present up to 18 months after the child's death. This
continued reaction to the unexpected loss of a child by
suicide is not the same as a grief reaction. Grief is a self-
limited process and does not lead to long impairment of one's
activities. The grief of these parents is not self-limited but
self-perpetuating and often interferes with his own activities
and the mental health of the entire family. This is more
characteristic of depression. There also appears to be a social
reaction to suicide. That is, most members of the society
appear to withdraw support from those mourning a suicide.
Friends and relatives find it impossible to talk about the
deceased and do not assist in helping the mourners work
through the loss. It was characteristic that these parents had
not been able to share their loss with family and friends. In
fact, it was our impression they had been unable even to talk
easily with each other.

Though these observations are preliminary, there can be
no doubt that the parents' adjusting to the death of their
child by suicide encounter considerable emotional turmoil,
much more, in fact, than has heretofore been substantiated.
The parents of children who commit suicide are plagued by
deep, unresolved guilt and prolonged periods of depression.
The fathers, especially, appear to need much help in adjusting to the suicidal death of their child.[7]

[7] *Ibid.*, p. 385.

The Surviving Community

In addition to the effect that a suicide has on the immediate survivors, it often has serious repercussions in the larger community as well. The well-publicized suicide of a famous person, a movie star or a popular political leader, for example, will often set off an epidemic of suicidal behavior in the general population. Many people who are having severe difficulties will see the famous suicide as being suggestive or as giving permission for similar behavior on their part. Suicidal depressions, threats, gestures, and attempts all seem to increase in the days following the suicide of a famous person. This is often a frightening experience for the person who feels the final restraints slipping away, and he normally hungrily reaches out for increased support during this time. He wants and needs reassurance that suicide is not the only solution to his problems and that help is available. The scope of this phenomena, the epidemic of suicidal behavior following the death of a famous person, is difficult to judge, and although some suicidal deaths unquestionably result, more often, the contagion takes the form of nonlethal suicide attempts, rather than death.

But the deceased does not have to be nationally renowned, in order to cause severe disquieting effects in his own immediate community. One example of this is the death of Rodger, a nineteen-year-old boy, who grew up in a lower middle-class neighborhood in Los Angeles. Rodger had always been accepted as one of the more quiet members of the crowd he ran around with. He was generally recognized as being smarter than most of the others, and that set him a little apart. Still, when he was accepted at the University of California, upon graduation from high school, everyone felt that one of "them" had made it, and they vicariously enjoyed the accomplishment. When he returned home for Christmas vacation, at the conclusion of the first successful quarter, people were glad to see him and were happy that he had done so well. No one expected that three days after his return he would be discovered dead by hanging in his parents' garage.

The reaction among his peers was first shocked unbelief. As the denial slowly passed, it was replaced with an insatiable hunger for information. What had happened? How? Why? For a few days, the young people could not be together enough. They needed the closeness, the support, the reassurance that everyone else was still there and that the world was progressing in spite of the earth-shattering event they had all experienced. Then the closeness began to dissipate as a general feeling of depression and isolation set in. Most of the young people began thinking about suicide; how it would feel. Would I ever try it? Under what circumstances? What means would I use? Several of the young people made vague suicide threats in the ensuing weeks, and one made an attempt with an overdose of pills. It took about six months for the students to return to normal —normal, but not the same.

The adult community reacted differently. The principal of the high school issued a memo to the faculty to the effect that since Rodger was no longer a student there the school held no responsibility for the unfortunate event, and no faculty member should involve himself in any way. When one teacher, who was closer to the children than most, requested some sort of memorial service to help the students with their feelings, the request was abruptly denied and the teacher admonished not to become involved. Angry feelings arose among the faculty as most felt constrained to take sides over the issue of whether or not this repressive approach was appropriate. For some, the school has never returned to normal. Feelings of anger, resentment, and fear are devisive, and the aftermath of a suicide often finds them all present and sometimes unresolved.

Many clergymen report a variety of unsettling experiences, both in their own churches and in their own communities after a suicide. The minister of a Methodist church in a small Oregon town found the whole community upset following the suicidal death of a popular local schoolteacher. The teacher was fifty-six years old and had been in the community for years, having taught many of the parents of the children who were now enrolled in her school. Guilt, fear, and depression became contagious as absurd rumors swept the community and people started to panic. Although the cause of death was clearly suicide, the teacher even having written a note, speculation of murder became rampant as people were unable to accept the fact that such a person could entertain such intensive depressive feelings that would lead her to take her own life. The specter of the mysterious intruder stalked the community for months after the death, and suspicion and accusation undermined the morale of the community as people in their anxiety attempted to assign blame and some rational cause for this inexplicable event.

In still another community, a fifty-year-old man, who had been active in the church for many years died by suicide. He had been the victim of intense, long-term depression for most of his life, and he had received years of psychiatric help. Although there were no overt suicide incidents reported as a result of this death, the reaction of this large metropolitan church indicated that the death was a traumatic one to the congregation. Some of the members of the congregation responded with overt anger toward the man and openly resented the fact that others were responding by idealizing him. Those who were angry recalled positions which he had supported on the official board of the church from years ago. His family expressed anger more subtly by flagrantly disregarding his wishes concerning the type of funeral he had wanted. Whereas he had requested a closed casket, cremation, and no graveside services, the actual funeral was characterized by an open casket, burial, and a graveside service.

Others in the congregation experienced a variety of feelings, from an open and compassionate expression of loss, to deep bewilderment and confusion that a "religious person" could die by suicide. Others wanted to deny that this was actually a suicide and openly sought reassurance that the death might have been caused by a heart attack or some other natural phenomena. Still others attempted to impute to the suicidal act virtuous motivations; one woman vocally proclaiming it as an act of rare courage, and another saying that it was a highly Christian thing to do in that it was a sacrificial death permitting a significant amount of insurance money to flow to his family.

A strong guilt reaction was also experienced by the congregation. This was manifested in a variety of ways including an overt and open expression of, "If I had known he had been feeling so badly I could have done something to help," to more covert expressions, such as the establishment of a memorial fund in his honor. Just five months prior to this suicidal death, another patriarch of the congregation had died a natural death, and the fact that there was no mention of a memorial fund at this time provides an interesting counterpoint.

The ministers of the church received some criticism by certain members of their congregation for not having helped this man more. The facts are that the man had received many hours of intensive psychiatric treatment and pastoral counseling and that he was not ignored by the minstry of the church. Such criticisms, however, are not unusual and reflect the anxieties of some people in their need for benevolent authority to have the power to prevent tragedy.

The funeral was an intensely difficult one and was characterized by major confusion, even in such routine areas of time schedules and the assignment of routine tasks. It was one of the largest funerals the church had ever had, many of the people responding to curiosity and anxiety that such a man would kill himself.

Helping the Survivor

As we have seen, being of help to the survivor in a suicidal death can be a very difficult and trying role. Survivors often react to their loss in strong emotional and even irrational ways. They frequently distort the facts of the death, and the emotional strain that they are living through makes it difficult for everyone around them and makes it very difficult to approach them in a helpful way. Still, with all these difficulties, it is equally obvious that such people are in need of help at this time, possibly more than any other time in their lives. It is the clergyman who often finds himself in the position of being the one person who can offer significant help, both as the officiating pastor at the funeral and in his role as a counselor.

The Funeral

Although the funeral of a suicide is difficult for everyone, it is the clergyman who has the most complex task. He must cope not only with his own intense feelings, but with the feelings of the immediate survivors and of the entire community. He must sometimes prepare a public statement on this highly taboo subject which he hopes will be helpful to all concerned. His professional role permits him no luxury of retreat into privacy. On the day of the funeral his office demands that he have something relevant and comforting to say. This is no easy task, and many clergymen look back on such an experience as being one of the most difficult in their ministry.

One of the factors that makes such an address so difficult is that many clergymen have not sufficiently worked through their own thoughts and feelings about suicide. They are uncertain if theologically suicide represents a sin, a sickness, or a free choice, and because of this confusion in their own thinking, they are uncertain if their attitude should be one of condemnation or forgiveness, regret or respect. The classical Christian view was that suicide was a sin, and as a sin, should simply be condemned. The church would simply withhold its compassion and not permit the rights of burial to the sinner. This attitude, although very hard on survivors, made the position a relatively easy one for the clergyman who did not have to deal with any ambivalence or conflict within himself but could simply follow the harsh rules of a legalistic church. Such is clearly not the case, however, in our own time. Not only have the church's rules softened considerably, but recent research indicates that most clergymen are retreating from the absolutist position and exposing themselves to the painful project of reevaluating what a suicide in the congregation means to them.[8] If it is a sin, most clergymen feel it is not necessarily unforgivable, and the question of implementing forgiveness and compassion becomes an important issue.

If it is a sickness, then the responsibility seems to fall hard upon the entire community which may have failed to diagnose the sickness in time and to respond with redeeming Christian love. The fact of a suicide completed, then, brings into question the responsibility of the whole church community and each individual's participation in his relationship with the deceased. Guilt becomes a major issue which cannot be ignored during the grieving process.

If suicide represents a free choice, then the question of the limit to free choice that Christianity can endorse becomes a serious question, and the obligation upon us all to be our brother's keeper comes into direct clash with the person's desire not to be kept. Should a funeral ever glorify or sentimentalize a suicidal death? Should the funeral address ever even hint that such a solution is acceptable to the Christian, thereby implying permission for subsequent suicides to follow?

These are important theological and emotional issues which every practicing clergyman sooner or later will have to face as he contemplates his funeral address for a suicided parishioner. Moreover, the clergyman will have

[8] Homer Demopulos, "Suicide and Church Canon Law" (doctoral dissertation, School of Theology, Claremont, California, 1968).

to address himself to the question of what this particular suicide means. Every suicide has its own unique emotional content and meaning to the survivors, including the clergyman. Especially in those cases where the clergyman was in direct contact with the deceased and knew something of the stresses and the failing coping mechanisms that he was experiencing, he will be closely involved. In such a case the clergyman's first priority is to sort out his own feelings, and to get in close touch with his own dynamics. We have seen how suicides frequently stimulate feelings of anger, resentment, and guilt in surviving people, and this is no less true of the clergyman. A suicide is often a dramatic rejection of people who have been concerned and who are trying to help, and it is only natural that the survivors will feel rejected and experience feelings of anger and frustration. The clergyman should realize that such feelings are normal and inevitable, and that once they can be consciously experienced they can usually be more appropriately handled.

Once his feelings are relatively under control, the second task that faces the clergyman is to make himself available to the family in an effort to determine what they are feeling and how they are reacting to this traumatic experience. He will probably observe the family on several levels. He will be aware of the kinds of defenses that they are employing to get themselves through a difficult time, and he will also be in touch with some of the deeper feelings that are present. It is important that the clergyman recognize the wide range of emotional reactions that are possible in such circumstances and that he confront the family in an accepting and nonjudgmental manner. Fortunately, few people have the experience of one woman who, after her husband's suicidal death, reported that her minister said, "that my husband was taken to punish me, and that he would probably never go to heaven because he had never been baptized."[9]

Hopefully, more typical is the response of another woman whose husband died of suicide. She characterized her minister as offering "calm encouragement without being maudlin"; or from still another woman, who said, "the message before and during the funeral was from his heart and helped us all in our loss"; or still another, who said her clergyman was instrumental in "making me realize that perhaps all is not lost after all."

Another factor which the alert clergyman will want to take into consideration as he goes about the task of preparing for the funeral is the emotional climate in the church and in the community. If it is a fairly large funeral with one hundred fifty or more in attendance, the clergyman can assume that there are several listening to him who have had serious suicidal thoughts and may even be actively contemplating suicide at this time. These people will be listening to him with acutely tuned ears, wondering what he has to say on this emotionally charged topic. They will be in a state of high vulnerability and may be on the brink of some action. What this action will be may depend, in large measure, on how they perceive the clergyman as he leads the congregation in the funeral service. If they perceive him as being a sensitive, accepting person, who offers alternatives other than death to perplexing problems, they

---

[9] Howard Stone, "The Grief Responses of Middle-aged Spouses: Suicide and Non-suicide Compared" (doctoral dissertation, School of Theology, Claremont, California, 1970), p. 44.

may well be encouraged to approach him for help. Such a response could be one indication that the clergyman has been able to turn a tragic situation into an avenue of significant help for other people.

Most clergymen will want to avoid either condemning or condoning suicide, just as they will want to avoid glorifying suicide, either directly, as being some kind of sacrificial act, or indirectly by oversentimentalizing the tragedy. Instead, they will want to treat the act of suicide as directly as they can under the circumstances. Some families cannot bear to face the fact of suicide within the short period of time from the death to the funeral. One such family was that of Mr. Valentine, a divorced man, living alone, who had been subject to lifelong depressions, who was unemployed and was feeling alienated and unloved by his family. One afternoon he took his .22 rifle and shot himself in the head. The family felt so guilty for having ignored him in the past few months and having been unresponsive to his weak and tentative cries for help that they could not bear to face the fact of suicide. Instead, they built up the case for a mysterious intruder, who came and killed him, although there was no direct evidence for such an event and the case was clearly a suicide. The clergyman handling the funeral, however, did not challenge them on this point, but instead made himself available as they tried to work with the feelings of this sudden tragic death. Several weeks after the funeral, the deceased's niece, in thanking the clergyman for the way things had been handled, told him that she guessed she knew all along that her uncle had killed himself but had just not been able to face it all at once. She appreciated not being "hit over the head" with the facts, being permitted instead to arrive at them in her own time.

Much of the reaction to the funeral of the suicide is beyond the clergyman's control. People bring their own needs and their own emotional sets with them to a large extent. Some people find the ritual of a funeral of great help, such as the lady who responded, "The funeral did make me feel better, seeing how nice he looked and so very peaceful, I felt slightly relieved"; and another lady who observed, "Over three hundred people came to his funeral. This made the children and I feel pretty proud"; and again, "I realized that I would now have to make a new life."

For others, however, the funeral is a difficult time, and they carry bad reactions away. One woman said, "I think the funeral was more depressing. I feel they should be abolished completely"; and another more dramatically observed, "It was a tribelike ritual and even though it was a closed coffin, the smell of flowers and the smell and look of grief was the most macabre and nauseous experience I've had. The experience clings around one like a musty drape. Death I can cope with—the capitalization I cannot."

Perhaps most peoples' experience, at such a time, was given expression by still another woman, who said, "I do not feel that the funeral helped me in any way. I was in a state of shock at the time. It was as if it weren't happening to me." The emotional trauma that the suicidal death of someone close can produce often results in the kind of detachment and dissociation that this latter woman was experiencing. For her, the whole funeral experience occurs as if in a dream, and she appears to others to be out of touch with what's happening. Such a person is delaying her grief reaction and should be watched carefully in the weeks following the funeral.

Counseling

Although each counseling situation is unique, carrying with it its own peculiar problems and opportunities for the pastoral counselor there are some basic principles that would be common to most such situations.

It is an axiom in most good psychotherapy that one should always respect the defenses of his patient. Although these defenses may be transparent to the therapist and although they may be causing considerable difficulty to the patient himself and to those around him, the therapist always needs to remember that the patient has erected the defenses for a purpose and the purpose is that he needs them, at least for the time being. The defenses, therefore, need to be respected and treated with care, and this axiom is equally true in the case of a suicidal death.

If the survivor needs, for the moment, to distort the facts, or to deny what is obvious to everyone—that his spouse, child, or friend has, in fact, killed himself—the minister will be doing great service if he can simply permit the distortion or the denial for the time, and not feel that he has to argue the person out of it or force him to face traumatic fatcs which he is seeking so desperately to avoid. This does not mean that the clergyman should encourage denial or the distortion, and it certainly does not mean that he should feed the counselee's need to find an "enemy," nor should he encourage displaced anger. But to the extent that the counselee needs some defensive conceptualization of what happened, the pastor should permit it, seeking neither to endorse it nor deny it, but just accept it as something that is needful for the time being.

This is true not only in conversations that the pastor will

be having prior to and subsequent to the funeral, but is also a good guide to follow in the funeral address itself. To make an issue of the fact that a suicidal death was a suicide when the family has been giving out clear signals that they need, for the moment, to disguise this would be unkind.

On the other hand, if those immediately involved have showed signs that they are able to accept the fact that a death was a suicide, it would be doing them no service to seek to avoid this issue, either in counseling or in the funeral address. The issue could be addressed directly as a fact.

A second general principle is that in the case of those who are having difficulty with their grief following a suicidal death the clergyman might take the focus off the suicide and onto the fact of death. Many survivors will tend to become obsessed with the question, "Did this person kill himself or not," or become obsessed with the fact that he did. The tendency with many survivors is to become so locked in with the issue of suicide that they are unable to progress with the normal grief work which is necessary following any death. The fact of suicide tends to obscure the fact of death in some cases, and to the extent that this happens, healthy grief work is made impossible. If the clergyman could focus his attention on the issues of loneliness, sadness, and the need to readjust one's life in terms of the continuing absence of a loved one, he will be serving a good purpose.

Although most suicidal deaths bring to the surface, in the survivors, deep and important emotional issues and needs, the time immediately around the suicidal death is not the time to go searching for deep insights. Although we have touched on some of the unconscious wishes and desires that make normal grief work difficult following a suicide, it would be inappropriate to try to make this kind of therapeutic gain in the face of an immediate loss. The third principle, therefore, is that the clergyman should see himself in a supportive role around the time of the funeral. It is a time for human warmth and support, not therapeutic interpretations or insight gathering. As the counseling relationship develops, and as time passes, the role of the counselor can shift from one of supportive crisis work to therapy orientated toward growth enhancement.

A fourth principle which might help to guide a clergyman's actions has to do with mobilizing whatever normal, social resources that the survivor has in his own life's sphere. Suicide is an anxiety-producing and even a traumatic topic for many people, and many respond to this anxiety by staying away. The clergyman can be of great help by aiding friends and relatives of the survivor to deal with their own anxieties in order that they can be more available to the person who now needs them the most. One way the clergyman can do this is simply by example. Mrs. King felt, rightly or wrongly, that she was being ignored, not only by her friends but by her pastor. It is difficult to tell to what extent this was factually true, and to what extent it was a figment of her own suspicion and unhappiness, but in either case, the clergyman should realize the importance of this issue and go out of his way to spend even more time with this kind of grief situation than he normally does. He can be encouraging to others, as well, to reach out in a caring way at this time.

Since the suicidal death does, however, bring up important emotional conflicts, professional aid is sometimes needed to help the person work through the consequences of his loss. Yet it is exactly at this time that many people feel most frightened and vulnerable, and it is difficult for them to seek out the kind of professional help they need. The clergyman can be very helpful in this kind of situation, not only by encouraging the survivor to seek professional help if he is unable to cope with his own grief process, but by actually taking the initiative to find the qualified professional person and help the survivor get to him. In many cases, the professional therapist will see the clergyman as being an important resource and will welcome the opportunity to work with him.

In some cases of a disturbed grief reaction, the survivor may be unwilling for one reason or another to seek professional help and yet be very open to working with the clergyman. This sometimes places the parish minister in the position of wanting to help someone but feeling that he is in over his head with dynamics which are too deep for a person with limited training. This was true in the case of Jack W., a nineteen-year-old boy, who had the misfortune of discovering his mother in her bathroom after she had shot herself with her husband's shotgun. Not only did the boy suffer the expected kinds of symptoms from such a traumatic discovery, but the situation was complicated by his anger toward the psychiatrist who had been seeing his mother, and by extension to all professional therapists. His mother had been under psychiatric care for several years and had been hospitalized twice for short periods of time. Jack had the experience of seeing his mother become progressively worse as her depressions deepened and other symptoms became more intense. The suicidal death was a climax to years of distress and worry. Jack felt that the situation was largely the fault of the psychiatrists who, he felt, "were nothing more than a bunch of witch doctors." In the months following his mother's death, Jack began to turn more and more to dope, became erratic on his job, and ran into trouble with the police three times. Jack's father was of little help to him, being locked in a serious reactive depression himself. He would go to work, come home, and sit staring blindly before the television set until late at night, and then repeat the process the next day. Although it was clear to everyone that both Jack and his father needed professional help, both shared the same resentment toward the entire profession. Jack's clergyman was the one professional person that Jack felt reasonably close to, although his father did not share this resource. The Rev. Mr. Johnson felt he was attempting to cope with a situation that was beyond his experience and training and yet, at the same time, felt that he was the only resource that the boy had. This situation was nicely resolved when Mr. Johnson sought consultation with a professional person who had some experience with suicide. Armed with this consultation support, he was able to maintain a helpful relationship with Jack for a long period of time and was of significant help in a difficult adjustment period.

Many survivors of suicides have an experience similar to Jack's in that they find that difficulties in the mourning process really begin when the funeral is completed. Even Mrs. King was able to get through the funeral well enough, and it was only later, as the days stretched into weeks and months that her real trouble began. Part of the reason for this is that many people who are involved with the stricken family tend to see the funeral as the end of the mourning process. Responding well for the few days between the death and the burial, they then feel that they are able to return to their normal routines and as a consequence the bereaved family feels ignored and isolated.

Continuing support is always a problem and one of which most clergymen are well aware. The problem, simply stated, is usually one of time. Time is a precious commodity for the busy minister and when faced with several families in the congregation who need extensive follow-up support, he often discovers that the time necessary for this is simply not available. Other alternatives need to be found. Where it is appropriate and possible, helping the bereaved family into some line of action is often a good idea. Frequently, the trauma of a suicidal death in the family will motivate the family to reemphasize the role of religion in their lives, and they will become active in the life of their church. This, of course, should be encouraged wherever possible, as such activity is not only beneficial to the church but is of great therapeutic value for the family itself.

Sometimes a special project grows out of a suicidal death. The case of the man who became active in the drug abuse movement in his own community has already been cited. In other communities, local suicide prevention centers and telephone helplines have been created and supported as a response to someone's tragic loss. These services, when they are well run and administered, provide a significant help to those who did not find the kind of help they needed at the time of their crisis. The clergyman can be of great significance in such a situation, helping the bereaved to assess his own talents and strengths, helping him to channel whatever concern and energy he has in the most appropriate way.

172

Recommendations

In the study by Herzog and Resnick, another finding was that almost all of the parents interviewed stated that they would have appreciated the help of a professionally trained person who could have talked with them about their feelings immediately at the time of the death. Yet, only one family interviewed sought professional help at the time of their loss, and this family turned to their minister.

The need for such professional contact by survivors of a suicidal death and the inability to take the initiative of searching it out provides an opportunity for clergymen and other concerned professionals. Herzog and Resnick suggested any community suicide prevention center might dispatch a trained professional to talk with a family within twenty-four hours of the suicidal death. If there is no suicide prevention center in the community to carry out this activity, the researchers suggest that the medical examiner–coroner's office have available such a professional. Since neither of these groups seems likely to implement this suggestion in the foreseeable future, clergymen might well be employed to offer such help. This would be especially true in those cases where the suicide took place within the congregation. The researchers go on to state that "optimal time for the initial contact with parents is within the first few hours of the child's death. At this time, most parents appear to be quite willing and even eager to talk to an understanding person who is not a part of the official inquiry. Not only does this early interview, in the opinion of the researchers, serve as a therapeutic and cathartic experience for the parents, it also allows the interviewer to establish rapport so that he can provide the parents with appropriate subsequent help." [10]

They also suggest that help for the family of an adolescent suicide could be offered in three phases. (1) psychologic resuscitation; (2) psychological rehabilitation; and (3) psychologic renewal.[11]

Psychologic resuscitation is the beginning of an attempt to help a family withstand their immense loss. It is suggested that the helper contact the family within twenty-four hours of the suicidal death. The purpose of this call would be to assist them with the initial shock of their grief. At this time, rapport would be established and a return visit within several days would take place. The basic emotional issues would probably include who is to blame, feelings of guilt, and hostility.

Psychologic rehabilitation would take place over the next few months, during which time concern for the unit integrity of the family would be manifested, the mourning process facilitated, and whatever social and emotional problems come to the fore would be dealt with.

From the sixth month on, there appears a phase of psychologic renewal. By this time, the family is once again gaining control of its integrity and help will be available only as they request it. Once the family is seen through the first anniversary of the death, an evaluation should be made as to what kind of long-term help, if any, will be needed.

This suggested course of response to a family suffering an adolescent suicide can serve as a tentative outline for ministers and other concerned professionals who are in contact with such a family.

[10] Herzog and Resnick, "Parental Response," p. 385.
[11] *Ibid.*, p. 384.

Chapter 5
Philosophical Foundations

Although scientific interest in the subject of suicide became active only within the last century, it would be a mistake to assume that the subject is new as a concern of mankind.

Interest in suicide is as old as recorded history, and it has usually elicited strong moralistic feelings from the community.

An historical survey of the major thoughts and attitudes toward suicide provides more than a history. It provides an appreciation of the wide range of thoughts and feelings that are very much alive and active today.

There is nothing exclusively ancient about the Pythagoreans, the Stoics, or the Epicureans, just as the punitive, oversimplified reactions of a John Wesley are far from dead.

An exploration of these attitudes then is at once an examination of the attitudes as they exist today and as they affect our response to the suicidal cry for help.

The Philosophical Approach

The Classical Philosophers

To the early Greeks, death was a terrible ending to life which held beauty and promise. Death was something to be avoided until the last possible moment. Choron summarizes the prevailing attitude in early Greek thought:

> Death is the greatest evil. "Gods so consider it," says Sappho, "else they would die." And Anacreon is terrified by approaching death: "Death is too terrible. Frightening are the depths of Hades. There is no return."
>
> The prevailing view of death could not appease this acute consciousness of mortality. Death was neither peaceful sleep nor the better and happier existence in the hereafter, although some held such views. Generally the dead were thought to become bloodless shadows wandering listlessly in the Underworld, which was more dreadful than anything known on earth.[1]

This conception of death is frequently expressed in Homer as in this statement of the shadow of Achilles:

> Speak not smoothly of death, I beseech you, O famous Odysseus, Better by far to remain on earth the thrall of another . . . rather than reign sole king in the realm of bodyless phantoms.[2]

There were other views of death present in the early Greek period, however. The Orphic brotherhoods had a different concept which found formal expression in the writings of Pythagoras. Choron summarizes this teaching:

[1] Jacques Choron, *Death and Western Thought* (New York: Collier, 1963), p. 32.
[2] Homer *Odyssey* (Great Books of the Western World; Chicago: Encyclopaedia Britannica, 1952), XI, 79.

He taught transmigration of the soul, its purification in the wheel of births, and its final reunion with the Divine. The soul is imprisoned in the body and leaves it at death, and after a period of purification re-enters another body. This process repeats itself several times. But to make sure that with every new existence the soul should retain its purity, or become even purer and better, and thus come ever closer to the final stage where the reunion with the divine takes place, man must follow a certain discipline. Philosophy becomes with Pythagoras a way of life that assures salvation.[3]

To Pythagoras, suicide is a rebellion against the gods. It is an action that stems from perturbation, which is a pollution of the soul, and therefore an unworthy act.

Socrates takes this view into account and endorses it.

The reason (against suicide) which the secret teaching (i.e., Pythagoras) gives, that man is in a kind of prison, and that he may not set himself free, nor escape from it, seems to be rather profound and not easy to fathom. But I do think, Cebe, that it is true that the Gods are our guardians, and that we men are a part of their property. . . . No man has a right to take his own life, but he must wait until God sends some necessity upon him as has now been sent upon me.[4]

Here, then, suicide is condemned as being a presumptive act of man, a transgression on the rights of the gods. It is only when the gods themselves have made their will known as being in favor of a specific suicide that man may act in this way.

Plato, too, denies the right of suicide as a general rule

[3] Choron, *Death and Western Thought*, p. 33.
[4] Plato *Phaedo* (Great Books of the Western World; Chicago: Encyclopaedia Britannica, 1952) , p. 233.

but then goes on to enlarge upon the nature of the conditions under which suicide may be acceptable.

And what shall he suffer who slays him who of all men, as they say, is his own best friend? I mean the suicide, who deprives himself by violence of his appointed share of life, not because the law of the state requires him, nor yet under the compulsion of some painful and inevitable misfortune which has come upon him, nor because he has had to suffer from irremediable and intolerable shame, but who from sloth or want of manliness imposes upon himself an unjust penalty. For him, what ceremonies there are to be of purification and burial God knows, and about these the next of kin should enquire of the interpreters and of the laws thereto relating, and do according to their injunctions. They who meet their death in this way shall be buried alone, and none shall be laid by their side; they shall be buried ingloriously in the borders of the twelve portions of the land, in such place as are uncultivated and nameless, and no column or inscription shall mark the place of their internment.[5]

Following in the same tradition, Aristotle condemns suicide on the grounds that it is a cowardly act:

To seek death in order to escape from poverty or the pangs of love, or from pain or sorrow, is not the act of a courageous man, but rather of a coward; for it is weakness to fly from troubles, and the suicide does not endure death because it is noble to do so, but to escape evil.[6]

[5] Plato *On Laws* (Great Books of the Western World; Chicago: Encyclopaedia Britannica), IX. 753.

[6] Henry Romilly Fedden, *Suicide: A Social and Historical Study* (London: Peter Davies, 1938), p. 74.

Aristotle also lays great stress on the belief that a man is fundamentally a property of the state and has no right to deprive the state of any of its property:

> Therefore the suicide commits injustice but against whom? It seems to be against the state rather than against himself; for he suffers voluntarily and nobody suffers injustice voluntarily. This is why the state exacts a penalty; suicide is punished by certain marks of dishonor, as being an offense against the state.[7]

In the tradition of Pythagoras, Socrates, Plato, and Aristotle, then, suicide is seen in negative terms as an act deserving of condemnation. This judgment, however, is not a blanket one, and there are exceptions under certain circumstances. Cicero expresses this:

> Where God himself has given a valid reason as He did to Socrates and . . . to Cato, and often to many others, then of a surety your true wise man will joyfully pass forthwith from the darkness here to the light beyond.[8]

Valerius Maximum agreed with this conception, and commenting on the suicide of Cato, remarked:

> (Cato) gave a noble lesson to mankind. How much superior in the opinion of all honest men is dignity without life to life without dignity.[9]

A second main tradition of Greek philosophy, that of the Epicureans, has a much softened opinion of suicide.

[7] Aristotle *Nicomachean Ethics* (Great Books of The Western World; Chicago: Encyclopaedia Britannica), I. 30.74.87.
[8] Cicero *Tusculanarum Disputationum* tr. Charles Anthem (New York: Harper, 1867).
[9] Quoted in Dublin and Bunzel, *To Be or Not To Be,* p. 187.

Death, for the Epicureans, was not the terrifying subject that it was to the other Greeks:

> So death, the most terrifying of all ills, is nothing to us, since so long as we exist death is not with us, but when death comes, then we do not exist. It does not concern either the living or the dead, since to the former death is not, and the latter are no more.[10]

Man is alive to enjoy life, and when life ceases to be enjoyable, there is no reason to continue to live. Lucretius, the Epicurean poet who himself was a suicide, expressed this Epicurean point of view:

> If one day, as well may happen, life grows wearisome, there only remains to pour a libation to death and oblivion. A drop of subtle poison will gently close your eyes to the sun, and waft you smiling into the eternal night whence everything comes and to which everything returns.[11]

Perhaps the most famous quote in regard to this view of suicide is that from Epicurus:

> Above all things remember that the door is open. Be not more timid than boys at play. As they, when they cease to take pleasure in their games, declare they will no longer play, so do you, when all things begin to pull upon you, retire.[12]

For the Epicureans, then, the "door is open." Life will be lived as long as it is enjoyed, but when the hope for happiness dims, the door to death is always open.

[10] Epicurus *Letter to Menoccus*, quoted by Fedden, in *Suicide: A Social and Historical Study*, p. 70.
[11] *Ibid.*, p. 69.
[12] *Ibid.*, p. 87.

Stoicism is the third major tradition of Greek philosophy. Suicide, for the Stoics, was permitted if the act was one of reason, will, and integrity. Suicide as a result of despair was weakness and represented failure. Seneca considered old age and sickness as possible rational reasons for committing suicide:

> I will not relinquish old age if it leaves my better part intact. But if it begins to shake my mind, if it destroys its faculties one by one, if it leaves me not life but breath, I will depart from the putrid or tottering edifice. I will not escape by death from disease so long as it may be healed, and leaves my mind unimpaired. I will not raise my hand against myself on account of pain, for so to die is to be conquered. But if I know that I must suffer without hope of relief, I will depart, not through fear of pain itself, but because it prevents all for which I would live.[13]

The major consideration for the Stoics was that the person be in rational control of whatever decision he makes:

> As I choose the ship in which I will sail, and the house I will inhabit, so I will choose the death by which l leave life . . . in no matter more than in death should we act according to our desire.[14]

Suicide, as an act of cowardliness, is condemned by the Stoics, but if it is executed in proper circumstance it can be an act of bravery:

> To death alone it is due that life is not a punishment, that, erect beneath the frowns of fortune, I can preserve my mind

[13] *Ibid.*, p. 76.
[14] *Ibid.*, p. 74.

unshaken and master of itself . . . I see the rack and the scourge, and the instruments of torture adapted to every limb and to every nerve; but I also see death . . . . She stands beyond my haughty fellow countrymen. Slavery looses its bitterness when by one step I can pass to liberty. Against all the injuries of life, I have the refuge of death.[15]

Perhaps the best summary of the Stoic attitude toward suicide is given by Tillich:

The Stoic recommendation of suicide is not directed to those who are conquered by life but to those who have conquered life and are able both to live and to die, and can choose freely between them. Suicide as an escape, dictated by fear, contradicts the Stoic courage to be.[16]

Philosophers of the Enlightenment

Many of the same points of view that were represented in the Greek philosophers were discovered and expressed again in the thinking of the Age of Enlightenment.

In his *Essay on Suicide* (1789), Hume stressed that right which everyone has to exercise his freedom of choice in deciding whether or not he shall continue to live. He refutes Aristotle's argument that every man owes it to society to remain alive, holding that a suicide does no harm to society, he merely ceases to do good. Man has the freedom and the right to dispose of his own life as he will, and this freedom is of primary concern. The purpose of this essay is to "restore men to their native liberty by examining all the common arguments against suicide and showing that

[15] *Ibid.*, p. 75.
[16] Paul Tillich, *The Courage to Be* (New Haven: Yale University Press, 1952), p. 12.

that action may be free from every imputation of guilt or shame." [17]

Joining with Hume in this emphasis on human liberty to do as one will with his own life was Montaigne who re-affirms the Stoic point of view.[18] Montesquieu also affirmed the right of suicide on the grounds that life is a blessing, and when it ceases to be desirable, one is free to give it up.[19] Voltaire too found the right of suicide in cases of extreme emergency to be an important right.[20]

Kant stood on the other side of the issue holding that all human life was sacred and must be preserved at all costs. He stressed that suicide is inconsistent with reason and inconsistent with his categorical imperative by which every act should be judged. The potential suicide should ask himself what would follow if everyone did what I am about to do.[21]

Goethe had compassion for the suicide and expressed admiration for Emperor Otho whom he felt committed suicide for a noble purpose. But Goethe felt that he would lack the courage to kill himself.[22]

Schopenhauer characteristically dwelt on the ills of life, but he discarded suicide as an answer to the problem. The suicidal person is not really desiring to reject life, he is

[17] David Hume, *An Essay on Suicide* (Yellow Springs, Ohio: Kahoe, 1929).

[18] Michel Montaigne, "That to Study Philosophy Is to Learn to Die" (Great Books of the Western World; Chicago: Encyclopaedia Britannica), Vol. VVX.

[19] Charles Montesquieu, *Persian Letters*, tr. John Davidson (London: George Routledge & Sons, 1901), letters 76, 77.

[20] Dublin and Bunzel, *To Be or Not To Be*, p. 218.

[21] Immanuel Kant. *The Metaphysics of Ethics*, tr. J. W. Semple (Edinburgh: T & T Clark, 1871), p. 239.

[22] Johann Wolfgang Goethe, *Poetry and Truth*, tr. Minna Steele Smith (London: G. Bell and Sons, 1913), II, 125-27.

rejecting the conditions under which he has been forced to live. He is, indeed, expressing a will to live in his rebellion against all the conditions of his life which limit his basic freedom to enjoy life.[23]

William James, as we have seen (Introduction, note 2), rejects suicide, holding that the human task is to find a religious meaning in our individual human lives. When this religious search is taken seriously, human life becomes meaningful.

Thus have the philosophers of both ancient and modern times struggled with the question of suicide in terms of what a man has a right to do with his own life. In the same vein, the major religions of the world addressed themselves to this question.

The Religious Approach

Just as there are numerous philosophical positions on the topic of suicide, so there is a broad spectrum of religious belief on the subject.

The Zuni tribe of North America knows of no suicidal behavior at all, whereas the neighboring Navaho have a religious belief-system which includes suicide as a ritual whenever the individual has broken one of the many taboos and has brought shame to himself. Among the Navaho, suicide is often an expression of revenge. It is as if the wronged person were saying, "Look what you have done to me." When this happens, then the community expects the original wrongdoer to take his own life as a payment.[24]

---

[23] Arthur Schopenhauer, *The World as Will and Idea* (London: Kegan, Paul, Trench, Tribune and Company, 1907).

[24] For a well-documented account, see Louis I. Dublin, *Suicide: A Sociological and Statistical Study,* (New York: Roland Press, 1963).

The strong belief in an afterlife among the Navaho is also an important factor in the high suicide rate. Servants and wives frequently suicide after the death of a master or husband in order to continue to serve him in the hereafter. Suicide will take place in preference to any physical mutilation so that the person may enter the realm of death with a complete body.

Marital problems and the shame of pregnancy out of wedlock are also common causes for suicide among the Navahos.

Many of the same motivations for suicide are seen among the Oriental religions. The Buddhist doctrine of the living soul encourages suicidal behavior among widows who want to join their husbands in death. The act of self-destruction also serves as a religious ritual among the Buddhists. Drowning in sacred rivers is a way of washing the soul clean, and burning is also a purifying act.

In China, financial insolvency, personal insult, slight offenses to sacred ancestors, and impending punishment for capital crimes are sufficient cause for one to take his own life.

In most primitive cultures where suicide is accepted as an expression of religious faith, many of the same motivations are found. Suicide is an expiation for guilt, revenge against a wrongdoer, an entrance into the afterlife, and a highly regarded act of religious devotion and spiritual superiority.

In Japan, for example, suicide has traditionally been honored as an act of high courage. The graves of persons who have died from self-inflicted injury are frequently honored and turned into shrines. *Hara-kiri* is a suicide carried out with great courage in obedience to high principles; *Junshi* is another type of suicide which takes place after the death of a master; and *Shinyu* is the name for the double suicide of lovers who can see no happiness or honor in this life apart from each other.

In strong contrast to these religious systems which include suicide as a religious ritual or approved social behavior, Islam expressly forbids it. The Koran is the only major religious scripture which explicitly renounces suicide. In the Hebrew-Christian tradition, religious attitudes in regard to suicide are more unclear and complex.

Judaism

The Jewish people, according to most available statistical data, have always enjoyed a very low suicidal rate. In speculating on the causes of this phenomenon Dublin hypothesizes that the traditional view of the sacredness of all human life, which ultimately was the property of the Creator rather than the person, was an important determent to suicide. For example, God was so angry with Onan for spilling his own seed on the ground rather than using it for procreation that he slew him (Gen. 38:8-10).

There are six accounts of suicide in the Old Testament, and all of them are simply reported as historical facts, without any judgment being attributed to them.

1. Abimelech mortally wounded in battle by a stone dropped by a woman, instructed his armor-bearer to slay him "lest men say of me 'a woman killed him' " (Judg. 9:54).
2. Samson pulled the Philistine temple down killing his enemies and himself saying, "let me die with the Philistines" (Judg. 16:28-31).
3. Saul fell upon his own sword "lest the uncircumcized

come and thrust me through, and make sport of me,"
after his defeat in battle. (I Sam. 31:1-6).

4. Saul's armor-bearer followed his master's example
   (*Ibid.*).
5. Ahithophel hanged himself when his betrayal of
   David to Absalom failed (II Sam. 17:23).
6. Zimri, victorious king, burned himself to death to
   pay for his sins, notably the murder of his master,
   Elah (I Kings 16:18-19).

Thus in biblical times, there seems to have been no
express law against suicide. The act is not prohibited in the
Ten Commandments, nor is it mentioned in the other
biblical legal codes. The commandment, "Thou shalt not
kill," was not interpreted at this time to include suicide,
and those cases of suicide mentioned in the Old Testament,
as we have seen, did not receive condemnation.

In the intertestamental period, two incidents of suicide
are reported. In II Macc. 14:41-46, Razis takes his own life
rather than be taken by his enemies; and Eleazar, a Zealot,
urged his thousand followers to kill themselves rather than
be taken captive. It is said that 960 people followed his
advice and his example. This mass self-slaughter took place
in A.D. 73.

It would appear from this that suicide, rather than capture, was being accepted as a custom of the Jewish armies.
Indeed, so close was this practice to being accepted as a
tradition that in the siege of Jotapata, when things were
going badly for the Hebrews, the soldiers of Josephus
pleaded with him to kill himself and instruct them to do
likewise. Josephus, however, refused to accede to their pleas,

and instead delivered a stirring speech. He records this portion of it:

> Oh, my friends, why are you so earnest to kill yourselves? Why do you set your soul and body, which are such dear companions, at such variance? It is a brave thing to die in war, but it should be by the hands of the enemy. It is a foolish thing to do that for ourselves which we quarrel with them for doing to us. It is a brave thing to die for liberty; but still it should be in battle and by those who would take that liberty from us. He is equally a coward who will not die when he is obliged to die. What are we afraid of when we will not go up and meet the Romans? Is it death? Why then inflict it on ourselves? . . . Self murder is a crime most remote from the common nature of all animals, and an instance of impiety against God our Creator.[25]

This eloquent speech is possibly the first expression of what has come to be accepted as the traditional Jewish view of suicide.

It is also in the writings of Josephus that we find the first indication of a suicide being refused orthodox burial. The body of one who had killed himself had to be carried to the grave after sunset, and it was buried without the usual rites. From this time on, Jewish thinking takes a firm stand against self-destruction.

When Rabbi Hananiah ben Teradyon was suffering martydom under Hadrian, he protected his mouth from the flames so that he would not hasten his own death, saying:

> It is better that he who has given me my soul should take it away, rather than that I should destroy it myself.[26]

[25] *Ibid.*, p. 175.
[26] *Ibid.*, p. 175.

The oral tradition of early Judaism is recorded in the Mishnah—a part of the Talmud—and was compiled in the first quarter of the second century. These words are found in the document:

> Whenever a person of sane mind destroys his own life, he shall not be bothered with at all.

Rabbi Ismael says:

> One chants over his body a dirge with the refrain: Woe be unto thee who hanged thyself.

Rabbi Eleazar answers:

> Leave him in the clothes in which he died, honor him not, nor damn him. One does not tear one's garments on his account nor take off one's shoes, nor does one hold funeral rites for him; but one does comfort his family for that is honoring the living.[27]

Here is expressed another fundamental position of the Jewish religion concerning suicide. That although one does not mourn or honor a suicide, neither does one judge him or abuse him. Furthermore, the survivors are comforted and helped in every way, they are not ostracized or punish As we shall see in the next section, this is a significant difference from some early Christian practices.

As time went on, the Jewish law regarding suicide continued to be redefined. The Semachot is a post-Talmudic treatise dealing with the rules of mourning for the dead. The complication by Rabbi Ebel Rabbati took its final

---

[27] *Ibid.*, p. 176.

form about the eighth century. In this document the term "suicide" is not used. In its place the phrase *meabed azme ladaat* is employed, which means "one who intentionally destroys himself." The implication of the use of "destroy" in the place of "kill" carries the meaning of everlasting annihilation. The term *ladaat* means "conscious and intentional, consent" or "free will." It includes two elements: that the act was free from any outside pressure, and that the spontaneity must be evident prior to the act. The effect of this wording was to define suicide in a very narrow way, and to allow a wide latitude in defining a death as something other than suicide.

Another definition of suicide was offered by Maimonides (1135-1204). A man is a suicide if he is not willing to break the dietary laws and the regulations concerning the Sabbath rather than forfeit his own life. The advice is given to run away if you can. Also it is the person's right to disguise his religion rather than die, but he cannot perform any overt act prohibited by the Law. This, however, appears to be a minority view and did not receive general acceptance.

The latest codes from the sixteenth century constitute the basis of contemporary practice of Orthodox Jews. There are three major provisions. First, suicide is described as the most wicked act. There should be neither rending of the garments nor mourning on behalf of the suicide. He should, however, be cleansed, dressed in shrouds, and buried. Secondly, every effort should be made to regard the act of a possible suicide as an act of murder, not suicide. Unless there is clear and unmistakable evidence that the death was the result of an act of self-destruction, the assumption shall be that the death was by result of murder. Finally, if a child should take his own life, it shall be considered that he did the act unwittingly, that it is not a suicide. This is also the interpretation applied for any adult if it was possible that the deed was prompted by madness or through fear of terrible torture. In these cases, he shall be treated as any ordinary deceased person.

The traditional Jewish viewpoint then has always been strongly against suicide, and the Jews have traditionally enjoyed a low suicide rate as compared to other religious groups. There are three elements that may account for this low rate: the Jewish concern for the sacredness of life; the clarity and severity of the law in regard to suicide; and the narrow definition of what constitutes a suicide.

Christianity

The attitude of the Christian Church toward suicide, like the Jewish attitude, took several centuries to become formulated. Suicide was a fairly common occurrence in the first century, being endorsed as we have seen by the Stoics, Epicureans, and the Cynics, yet the New Testament makes no direct comment about it. The only suicide reported in the New Testament (unless the death of Jesus is defined as a suicide) is that of Judas. Only Matthew (Matt. 27:3-5) reports it, and he without comment, judgment, or elaboration. Some New Testament phrases appear to discourage suicide, such as Jesus' comment: "He who endures to the end will be saved" (Matt. 10:22 RSV) ; and some of Paul's teachings, for example, "If I give away all that I have, and if I deliver my body to be burned, but have not love, I gain nothing" (I Cor. 13:3 RSV) .

Yet there were two types of suicidal behavior that received the approval of the Christian community in the early years. Martyrdom was deemed a worthy act, commenting as it did on the cruelty of the pagan world, the lack of fear of death, and the strength of faith. Cyprian writes that true Christians did not fear death and willingly gave their blood to escape from a cruel world. Tertullian, in defense of martyrdom, cites with approval some well-known suicides, including those of Lucretia, Dido, and Cleopatra. Early Christian history is filled with stories of the faithful seeking out martyrdom as a sure means of eternal salvation.

The second class of suicides which were approved by the early church community were women who took their own lives rather than lose their chastity. Pelagia, a girl of fifteen, jumped from a roof to her death to escape a Roman soldier, and was canonized for her act. Ambrose said of her, "God was not offended by such a remedy, and faith exalted it."

Two other examples of such suicide include the death of Domnia and her two daughters who accepted drowning in preference to loss of chastity, and Belsilla, a twenty-year-old nun, who abused herself until she died, and in so doing received the approval of Jerome.

The first clear statements against suicide in the Christian tradition came from the pen of Augustine who in the *City of God* supported the view that suicide is never justified. He supports the opinion on the basis of four reasons. First, the Christian is never without hope as long as the possibility of repentance remains alive, but with suicide the possibility of repentance is gone. Secondly, suicide is homicide, and this is a forbidden act. Thirdly, there is no sin that is worthy of death. The Christian is not his own judge, for this is a prerogative of God alone. Finally, suicide is the greatest sin of any choice. The Christian is better advised to make any choice other than that of killing himself, for he will be guilty of a lesser sin, and still be alive to repent.

Augustine had to modify his position to some extent, since the Church had already canonized some suicides such as that of Pelagia. Augustine handles this by assuming that Pelagia had received a special divine revelation which sanctioned her act, but this was an exceptional case and did not invalidate Augustine's reasoning.

Augustine's view prevailed in the Church, and by the fifth century suicide was deemed an ecclesiastical crime by order of the Council of Arles in 452. This was the first time that suicide was considered by an official church body. In the following centuries the Church's view of suicide became more strict and punishment more intense. The Council of Orleans in 533 denied funeral rites to a suicide; the Council of Borage in 563 endorsed the prior council's action and further legislated that a suicide could not have the benefit of Mass. The Council of Auxerre in 578 again reaffirmed the stand, and the Council of Antisidor in 590 barred any gifts from suicides.

In the year 750, the fifth chapter of the *Penitential* of Egbert, Archbishop of York, denies burial to a suicide, "if they do it by the instigation of the devil." The fifth of the canons published in King Edgar's reign in 960 stated the same punishment "if they do it voluntarily at the instigation of the devil."

The Council of Nimes in 1284 confirmed all prior legislation and renewed the athema on suicides, and further stated that under no circumstances could a person who killed himself be buried on holy ground. No significant change has been made since this legislation. The Roman Catholic

Church still demands excommunication of the suicide and the forfeiture of all ecclesiastical rights and benefits.[28]

After Augustine, the next major theologian to consider at length the question of suicide was Thomas Aquinas. He called suicide a sin and a crime and based his judgment on three major points. First, everyone loves himself and therefore suicide is against nature and charity. Secondly, an act of suicide does injury to the community. This, of course, is a restatement of Aristotle. Finally, suicide is to be condemned because it assumes God's prerogative who alone has the right to give life and take it away. Thomas based his view of suicide on three basic Christian beliefs, the sacredness of human life, the importance of submissiveness to God, and the importance of the moment of death.

Protestantism reflects much the same attitude toward suicide as was manifest in the Roman Catholic Church. For example, in 1603 the Book of Common Prayer of the Church of England specifically denied the right of church burial to any "that have laid violent hands upon themselves."

The feeling against suicide ran even stronger in the minds of the people than in the writings of the theologians and councils. Throughout much of Christian history from the fifth century up to as late as the nineteenth, the corpse of a suicide suffered the greatest of indignities. Not only was the suicide denied a church burial, and denied the right to bequeath his personal property to his heirs, but the rage of the community was loosed upon the corpse. Frequently, in both England and Europe, the body was dragged through

---

[28] Codex Iuris Canonici Pii X Pontificis Maximi Iussu Digestus Benedicti Papoe XV Auctoritate Ptomulgatus. Romae, Typis Polyglottis Vaticanis, 1917. Canons 985, 1240, 1241, 2339, 2350.

the streets face down. It then was hung on a gallows and allowed to rot there or be devoured by the birds of prey. At other times it was dumped, unburied in an open field, or perhaps buried at a crossroads with a stake driven through its heart.

Superstition and fear surrounded the body of one who had killed himself. If the death took place in a house, the body could not be carried out through a door. It had to be removed through a window, or a portion of the wall was knocked out and then replaced. In Scotland it was belived that if the body of a suicide was buried within sight of the sea or any cultivated land, it would be disastrous to fishing or agriculture.

In Europe the bodies of stillborn infants, suicides, and excommunicated persons were buried (if at all) "out of sanctuary," that is, on the north side of the graveyard. This custom stemmed from the fact that it is from the north side of the church where the Gospel is read to recall sinners, as compared to the south side from which the Epistle is read to instruct the faithful.

Perhaps we can gain a sense of the feeling about suicide and its prevention as it was being expressed in the eighteenth century, through this quotation of John Wesley:

It is a melancholy consideration, that there is no country in Europe, or perhaps in the habitable world, where the horrid crime of self-murder is so common as it is in England! One reason of this may be, that the English in general are more ungodly and more impatient than other nations. Indeed we have laws against it, and officers with juries are appointed to inquire into every fact of the kind. And these are to give in their verdict upon oath, whether the self-murderer was sane or insane. If he is brought in insane, he is excused, and the law does not affect him. By this means it is totally eluded; for the juries constantly bring him in insane. So the law is not of the least effect, though the farce of a trial still continues. . . .

But how can this vile abuse of the law be prevented and this execrable crime effectually discouraged?

By a very easy method. We read in ancient history that, at a certain period, many of the women on Sparta murdered themselves.

This fury increasing, a law was made, that the body of every woman that killed herself should be exposed, naked in the streets. The fury ceased at once.

Only let a law be made and rigorously executed, that the body of every self-murderer, Lord or peasant, shall be hanged in chains, and the English fury will cease at once.[29]

Yet, even in the midst of such strong and even brutal feelings against suicide, some more moderate voices were heard pleading for temperance. John Donne, Bishop of St. Paul's in the mid-seventeenth century, wrote a book with the title of: *Biathanatos: A Declaration of That Paradoxe or Thesis that Self Homicide is Not So Naturally a Sin that it may Never Be Otherwise. Wherein the Nature and the Extent of All Those Lawes Which Seeme to be Violated By This Act Are Diligently Surveyed.*

Donne's thesis is that the power of God is great enough that we are in error in assuming that all suicides are irremissible sin. It was one of the first pleas for moderation and understanding. As a result of such writings, and because of the influence of such secular writers as Hume, Montaigne, Montesquieu, Voltaire, and others both custom and law began to be modified.

[29] John Wesley, *Works*, Vol. XIII, p. 481.

In England, for example, the last body to be dragged through the streets and buried at a crossroads was in 1823. In July of that year, a law was passed prohibiting the practice. In 1882 the legislature ordered that a suicide may have a normal burial, and in 1870 the forfeitures were removed. In 1882 a suicide was no longer a murder but only a misdemeanor. Society was becoming more lenient and less punitive.

The evolution of the Christian view of suicide, then, may be traced in this broad way. From a very permissive, unconcerned position in its earliest years, Christianity gradually built up an intense, punitive denunciation of suicide, and finally in the last century, modified its intensity while maintaining its disapproval. Historically, the Church sought to prevent suicide by condemning it as a sin, bringing its influence on secular authority to have suicide labeled a crime, permitting or encouraging atrocities against the corpse, and by threatening eternal punishment.

How effective these means of suicide prevention were cannot be proved. It does appear, however, that during the Middle Ages the suicide rate in Europe was negligible. Dublin feels that the strong stand of the Church was influential:

> ... when we review the history of suicide during the centuries we find that religious probibition acts as a strongly deterring influence. Bitter religious opposition, the force of condemnatory public opinion, and the severe penalties of the law were so effective that few people had the temerity to take their own lives.[30]

[30] Dublin and Bunzel, *To Be or Not To Be,* p. 210.

Durkheim, however, explains the low suicide rate during this period in another way. The main factor was that Europe at this time was a forcibly integrated community, and this is the primary antisuicidal factor. As we have seen, Durkheim was pessimistic about the hope that religion, as such, can have much of an influence on the suicide rate. If religious doctrine has any effect at all, which he doubts, it is at too high a price. "Religion modified the inclination to suicide only to the extent that it prevents man from thinking freely." [31] When a man is denied the right of free thought, when he is forced to accept a certain system of dogma, he does not have to face certain ultimate questions of his own existence, an he is spared the possibility of despair. He may be less suicidal, but according to Durkheim, he is also less a man.

There are the possibilities, then, that Christianity has exerted an antisuicidal influence on its adherents because it authoritatively prohibited suicide; it presented an integrated community; and because it presented man with a frame of reference, a Weltanschauung, in which he can live without facing existential questions.

On the other hand, there is the possibility that Christianity constitutes a suicidal incentive in that it has historically spoken in glowing terms of an afterlife, martyrdom has been seen as a sure way to salvation, and it has often been pessimistic about this world.

Before we conclude this section, we would allude to another possibility of religion as an antisuicidal factor. Paul Louis Landsberg was a victim of Nazi persecution who had planned to suicide if captured by the Gestapo. Once cap-

[31] Durkheim, *Le Suicide*, p. 375.

tured, however, he had a religious experience which he describes with the phrase, "I have now met Christ." He destroyed the poison with which he had planned to destroy himself and lived through the concentration-camp experience supported by his religious belief. He speaks of it in this way: "Suicide thrusts us back upon the mother's breast. It is infantilism. On the other hand, Christ guides us through struggle and suffering towards a brighter life.[32]

[32] Paul Louis Landsberg, *The Experience of Death* (London: Rockliff Publishing Corp., 1953), p. 134.

Chapter 6
The Rational Suicide

Criteria for Judgment

It was in summer of 1961 that Ernest Hemingway, depressed and upset about many things, including the conviction that he could never write again, placed a favorite shotgun in his mouth and pulled the trigger. It was an act consistent with his philosophy that man can be destroyed but should not be defeated; or as he himself once expressed it to Hotchner, "Hotch, if I can't exist on my own terms then existence is impossible. Do you understand? That is how I've lived, and that is how I must live or not live." [1]

"Torch Number One" the name twenty-one-year-old Jan Palach gave himself in his suicide note which was found after he burned himself to death in Wenceslas Square in downtown Prague. Acting to save Czechoslovakia from the "edge of hopelessness," Palach was protesting censorship of the indigenous press, and the presence of the Soviet occupation newspaper, *Zpravy*. The incident is reminiscent of the

[1] A. E. Hotchner, *Papa Hemingway* (New York: Random House, 1966), p. 328.

action of Norman Morrison, a Quaker, who in 1965, died of self-immolation in front of the Pentagon protesting the war in Vietnam.

Nicholas Z., a lonely, seventy-eight-year-old Polish immigrant, writes a sad letter home, concluding with this paragraph:

> I am sick and tired of the constant enemas I get and my stomach hurts, and my left hand can't lift anything. It seems I will remain a cripple, and if with such bad health one has to suffer (and my left side hurts very much), in order not to be a burden to anyone I decided to do away with myself.

He was later found dead by a bullet discharged from the gun held in his one good hand.

The clinical problem of whether these suicides *could* have been prevented has been the subject of most of this volume. The philosophical and ethical questions, however, of whether a suicide always *should* be prevented is one that has received comparatively little attention in contemporary literature. One reason for this may be that most professional persons who are interested in the question of suicide are already committed to its prevention and for them the issue has been resolved.

But for many other professionals, the answer to the ethical question: How far is a professional person to go in preventing a suicide? depends upon how the prior philosophical questions are answered: Does anyone or everyone have the right to kill himself? Is there such a thing as a rational suicide?

There are four types of suicides which our society often endorses as being rational and in regard to which the ethics of intervention might be open to question.

1. Those suicides carried out for the good of some cause, as in the case of religious martyrdom, military heroism, or dramatic social witness.

2. Those carried out as a reaction to what appears to be a literally hopeless, painful, and debilitating situation, as in the case of lingering terminal illness.

3. Those in which the circumstances are not desperate, but in which the individual is no longer receiving the pleasure from life that he wants and so makes the decision to go through the open door away from life. Ostensibly the death of Hemingway might fall into this category.

4. The so-called love-pact suicide where the double death is seen as having some aesthetic value, possibly being an expression of love, beauty, or dedication.

Some clinical illustrations of each of the categories may be helpful:

What we have designated as suicide in support of a cause, Durkheim described in terms of the altruistic suicide. Such a suicide, according to Durkheim, takes place when a person is overintegrated into his society and subordinates his own desires to the will of the group. One example of this is that of a captain going down with his ship to certain death in obedience to the social tradition that expects such behavior. Another example is that of the young man who died of self-immolation in Washington, D.C. as part of his protest against the war in Vietnam. Norman Morrison was thirty-two years old, married, and a father. He was a college graduate and also held a degree from a recognized theological seminary. People who knew him described him in terms of his capacity to be a close personal friend, profound in his thinking, and sensitive to human suffering. They deny that he was an eccentric or a fanatic.

But in fact he was a normal person in that he was genuinely concerned with other human beings, those in Vietnam and those who were with him. He was flattering to others as a conversationalist because he took what one had to say as something very important. Norman wasn't just a good listener but was truly concerned about the concerns of others. He loved people not in the sense of polite liberal abstractions but in the sense that other people got inside and affected him. He enjoyed carpentry around the house, gardening, softball, ice hockey, the things we all find normal. He was not a pious saint attempting some kind of fanatical purity.[2]

Morrison was a Quaker, and as such believed in a concerned and loving God, the sacredness of human life, and he exhibited the traditional Quaker abhorrence of war. We have then available to us a rather clear picture of Morrison's philosophical orientation, and a clear rationale for the act of self-destruction that he performed. If this were all that there is to say, Morrison could be cited as one of the rational suicides which comes about through dedication to some cause. What is missing, however, is a complete analysis of Morrison's personality development and a thorough appraisal of any psychiatric symptoms that might have been appearing in the last few years. What is needed, then, before any kind of accurate judgment might be made about the rationality of this type of suicide is more complete data so that a more thorough evaluation can be made from several points of view.

[2] "Memorial Service for Norman R. Morrison," Friends Coordinating Committee on Peace, November 21, 1965.

The second type of suicide which our society may consider to be rational and ethical is that which stems from what appears to be a hopeless situation. The prototype for this is the person, often elderly, who is suffering from a chronic, painful, and terminal disease. What is surprising to most people is that the suicide among this part of the population is as rare as it is.

One case which might serve as an example of this kind of situation is that of Joan S., an attractive twenty-four-year-old girl who has been suffering from Hodgkins disease since the age of twelve. The progress of the disease has been slowed down but yet continues with no real hope of a cure.

Joan had been married for four years to a man by whom she was pregnant prior to their marriage and who continued to have numerous affairs of which Joan was aware. She felt unloved by him and described her home situation as intolerable. Joan had affection for her 3½-year-old son, but she also felt that he deserved a mother who would be alive throughout his childhood and adolescence. She had strong feelings of self-depreciation and feared that anyone with whom she was closely involved would somehow be infected by her. She had thought about terminating her very unsatisfactory marriage but felt that her son deserved a father, even an inadequate one, and didn't know what she would do if she did divorce this man. It would be unfair of her to consider marriage to any man.

In addition to her husband and her son, there were a mother, a stepfather, and a sister. The stepfather paid very little attention to her. Her mother, on the other hand, was a very "sweet" long-suffering woman. However, the relationship was double-binding, for Joan felt strong dependency toward her mother, and yet felt trapped and unable to cope with the kinds of demands that her mother subtly made on her. Her sister, a widow, struggled to support herself and three children. Joan and her sister had a fairly good relationship, but Joan felt guilty about accepting any help from this sister who had problems of her own. Joan had been suicidal for several years and made two very serious attempts in a six-month period, both of which required hospitalization. She thought of herself as nothing but a burden to those near her and felt helpless and hopeless about ever attaining any significant degree of self-sufficiency and independence. The world, in general, and her son, in particular, would be better off if she were to die immediately and not burden everyone with several more years of emotional and financial stress. Her fantasy was that if she were to kill herself, her husband soon would remarry and her son would have a better mother almost regardless of whom the husband married.

In this case, as in the case of many such "hopeless" situations, the hopelessness, it later became clear, was more a result of Joan's emotional attitude than of the reality of the situation. After her repeated suicide attempts, Joan was placed in therapy and with the help and support of the therapist was able to make certain decisions which changed the complexion of her life entirely. She left her husband, moved in with her sister, and began to reorientate her life around finding satisfactions for herself. She made appropriate and realistic plans for her own social life, accepted certain financial and social responsibilities that gave her a feeling of self-sufficiency and ability, and was able to continue functioning effectively as a member of the family and of society. To be sure, it might be expected that Joan will experience future crises in which she will seriously consider suicide, but if this happens, it will be the result of her emotional situation rather than a rational decision.

The third type of suicide which some consider rational concerns the exit through the open door of the Epicureans when life has failed to provide sufficient satisfaction to justify continuation of life, even though there is no overt or physical, hopeless situation. One example of such a type may be that of Ernest Hemingway, referred to earlier. Another example is that of Mr. Johnson, a sixty-year-old man whose wife had passed away several months earlier from cancer. The Johnsons had been married for some thirty-five years, and although the marriage was childless, it was described by Mr. Johnson as being a very close and a very happy marriage. He was steadily employed at one of the large manufacturing firms in the area where he held a position of a skilled laborer. Four months prior to his wife's death they were told she had cancer and was given six months to a year. At that time Mr. Johnson retired from his position at the manufacturing plant in order to be at home and to nurse his ailing wife. When she died two months later he found himself without a job and without his wife—without his two main reasons for living. Being unable to tolerate the feelings he experienced in the house where they had lived for so many years, he sold the house and purchased a trailer in a senior citizens' park.

Mr. Johnson, himself, was in excellent physical health, had some interests, some hobbies, and was even able to formulate some plans for how he would spend his remaining years. He had no other family left, but had a close relationship with his wife's family. The problem was, as he put it, that he found no pleasure in anything anymore. He was chronically depressed and was unable to work through his grief. Life was flat and meaningless, and although there was no physical or mental agony, neither was there any pleasure or satisfaction in life. He began ruminating about suicide, considering several different plans. One night he came to the decision that life for him was no longer worth living, that he could no longer receive any satisfaction or pleasure, and so he killed himself.

The fourth category of so-called rational suicide is that which we have called the love-pact suicide in which the double death is seen as having some aesthetic value. Although not uncommon in romantic literature, such suicides are relatively rare in Western culture. They are more common in Far Eastern literature which characteristically portrays a pattern involving

"a young merchant or craftsman and a young girl." Because of economic difficulties, problems preventing their marriage, such as their parents' or spouses' objections, poor living conditions such as pending criminal proceedings or inadaptability to rapid social change, one night in spring or summer of the Tokyo-Osaka area toward dawn, they stab themselves (occasionally hang or drown themselves) and almost never survive.[3]

The actual love-pact suicides in Japan, however, do not usually follow this romantic picture. According to Dr. Ohara's study, these suicides are characterized by unstable

[3] K. I. Ohara and D. E. Reynolds, "Love-Pact Suicide" (manuscript).

job situations, unsatisfying sexual relationships, social, economic, and emotional difficulties. Far from being a high expression of beauty or dedication, they can be more accurately described as being desperate and unhappy resolutions of painful conflicts. Parties to a love-pact suicide are not dissimilar to people who commit suicide under less romantic circumstances.

One type of the love-pact suicide is the murder-suicide pact where one party seeks to take a "loved" one into death with him. One such case involved an attractive thirty-five-year-old mother who shot her ten-year-old son and then killed herself after writing a twenty-two-page suicide note expressing her fears for herself and her son, and explaining at some length that this seemed to her to be the kindest thing to do and the only way to resolve the conflicts that life offered. But again, clinical investigation into the life of this person revealed the increasing and intensifying symptoms of schizophrenia, terrible confusion and fear, paranoid ideation, and suspicion that had its climax in a double tragedy.

There are several major social and psychological factors that should be taken into account when the question of rational suicide is being considered.

The first element stems from the fact that no man lives in social isolation from his community. John Donne observed "No man is an island," and the disposition that one makes of his own life inevitably affects other persons. The question, Does a man have a right to commit suicide? for example, can never stand apart from the question, How would this suicide affect the survivors?—not only the immediate family, but also the wider community which usually sees itself as having a vested interest in every human life. Clinical evidence gathered in the last decade clearly indicates that a suicidal death inevitably complicates the process of mourning for those who are left, and if children are among the immediate survivors, they often never fully recover from the scars of the emotional trauma.

A second factor has to do with the psychological aspects of the motivation for suicide. Research into the causes of suicide indicates that psychological motivations for suicide are never unitary. Ambivalence is always present. The mutually contradictory wishes, to live and to die; to be rescued and to be abandoned; are always present. In the light of this one cannot assume that such words as, "I want to die," entirely express the state of the patient's mind at the time. Clinical experience indicates that in most cases, the words "I want to die" can more accurately be understood as intending to communicate the message "I need help", or "I am feeling desperate." The professional person who simply accepts at face value the literal meaning of a depressed person's suicidal communication would be destructively naïve. The other side of the suicidal person's wish must be uncovered and recognized as being an important part of the individual's total psychological makeup.

Another psychological factor to be considered in determining the rationality of suicidal intention is the effect that depression has on thinking and decision-making processes. When clinical depression becomes acute, mental tunnel-vision is common. A depressed person is emotionally incapable of perceiving realistic alternative solutions to a difficult problem. His thinking process is often limited to the point where he can see no other way out of a bad situation than that of suicide. A more objective evaluation of his situation can usually provide a variety of other viable solutions. Under such circumstances it should be clear that the individual is emotionally incapable of making a responsible decision as to whether or not to kill himself, and any suicidal decision he may make under these circumstances is clearly more a function of depression than of rational thinking. Any case for a rational suicide would have seriously to consider these factors.

Dilemma of the Counselor

The ethical question of whether or not to interfere with a suicide plan often arises in one of three specific contexts. The first is the issue of betraying a confidence. Most people assume, and most professionals hold sacred, the right of privileged communication to one's physician, priest, lawyer, or confidant. But what does such a professional person do when, after being sworn to secrecy, his patient proceeds to tell him of his suicidal thoughts, feelings, or plans, and then forbids him to make any communication to others who might be of significant help in preventing the act of self-destruction? It is not unusual, for example, for a high school counselor to be sworn to secrecy by an adolescent who then proceeds to confide in him suicidal thoughts and plans. The counselor is then left to feel the excruciating conflict of wanting to interfere with progression of the suicidal plan, and at the same time, respect the confidence that the adolescent has shown in him. Clinical experience clearly indicates that suicidal activity ferments best in an atmosphere of secrecy and collusion, and it is often only when concerned people are made aware of the situation and given the opportunity to react that the suicide potential drops.

What then is the counselor to do when faced with this dilemma? Does he proceed to be true to his principle and maintain his silence, or does he forsake this and move more directly to mobilize the adolescent's resources? The question is partly resolved if the counselor can take seriously the clinical evidence of ambivalence discussed earlier, and realize that one side of the student's personality is crying for help and is asking the counselor to be his voice in informing others of his desperate state. When the two alternatives are placed side-by-side in a forthright way: Which is more important, the preservation of an abstract principle or the saving of a life? the question almost seems to resolve itself. Unfortunately, what frequently happens is that, faced with the dilemma, the counselor reacts with anxiety and denies or represses the seriousness of the situation and fails to take the communication seriously with the result that the student has once again failed to communicate with a potentially helping person.

A second issue around which clinical complications often appear is that of property rights. Most suicidal people choose a specific method by which they plan to kill themselves, and the instrumentation of this plan is vital to them. Yet many professionals show great hesitance in taking from the suicidal person the instrument of his choice or, having taken it from him for a short period, appear too willing to return it to him. Many times suicides have been completed with the pills or the gun which had been returned to the patient because someone was respecting the ethical principle of property rights.

A third and perhaps more complicated clinical issue is the question of hospitalization enforced against the protestation of the patient who invokes his civil right not to be incarcerated. The law carefully protects patients from unjust or unnecessary incarceration either in jails or in hospitals, yet several times during their professional lives, most physicians and are faced with the problem of dealing with a patient who is not psychotic and yet who is highly suicidal.

Although hospitaliaztion is no guarantee against suicide, as most hospital administrators painfully realize, it often does provide a safer environment for a highly suicidal person than the loneliness of his own apartment or house. The ethical dilemma that the clinician faces is how to provide a safe environment for a patient who rejects the offers of help that the clinician is making. How far should a professional go in forcing conditions upon a patient against the patient's will for the purpose of protecting him against himself? Too many times when a person's civil rights have been respected disaster results, as, for example, when a highly suicidal drunk is released from jail upon the insistence of his family, only to continue with his suicidal plan. Although the necessity for physical restraint is relatively rare in suicidal cases, when the necessity is apparent, professionals are sometimes immobilized by what they conceptualize as the conflict between invading a person's private rights and protecting him against an impulsive death.

In the vast majority of suicidal situations then, it can be clearly stated that the determination to suicide is the result of a focus of stress that temporarily distorts the individual's ability to make rational decisions, and he needs to be protected from himself even over his resistance.

One argument against such suicide prevention holds the

position that man must be free in order to develop his own potential. He must be free even to make errors, and no one has the ethical right to enforce an external will on anyone else. What this argument overlooks is the finality of the suicidal act. In most life situations we do have the opportunity of learning from error. We have the luxury of saving ourselves from the consequences of our own decisions. We learn to equivocate, to hedge our bets, to change horses in midstream, to trust in fate, and to avoid decisions in a wide variety of ways. For the most part, we get by with this indecisiveness, sometimes having our cake and eating it too, and sometimes missing out entirely. But even when we miss, tomorrow is another day and, as someone once said about the British Empire, we somehow manage to muddle through.

When the issue is suicide, however, these equivocations are no longer possible. Suicide is a final act which allows no other day to undo what we have done, and an entirely new philosophical and ethical situation is before us. Once one places the loaded revolver to his head, the equivocations, inconsistencies, ambivalances all take on a plus or minus, black or white, polar quality. At this point, the facts are, I will either die or I won't, and there is no room now for equivical ethics or for indecisive action.

The Will to Suicide

The ethical question, then, is easily resolved when it can be determined that the suicidal person is not making a rational decision. When it becomes clear that depression or anxiety is distorting his thinking, or that his suicide would deeply affect the rights of the other people, other ethical concerns must take second place, and suicide prevention becomes the dominant ethical concern. But the issue before us now is whether or not there is a will to suicide which is not a function of ambivalence, depression, stress, symbolism, communication, or other ploys of the human psyche. Are there circumstances under which one can rationally, appropriately, clearmindedly make a decision to kill himself and be proud of it? Are there ever circumstances under which a clearminded, rational second person would agree and permit the final act to take place?

This will to suicide, if it exists, must be distinguished from a more generalized will to die, which is essentially passive in nature, and is seen often among the elderly and the very sick. The striving for survival is relinquished, and the person, simply waits, sometimes for years, for his bodily energies to dwindle or for the infection to conquer, so that he can cease to exist. The will to suicide, in contrast to this, is active in nature and time-specific. Instead of relinquishing, ceasing to struggle, and waiting patiently for death to come, the will to suicide is active, in control, and takes the initiative in terms of method and time performing deliberately the action that leads to immediate death.

The will to die can also be distinguished from a willingness to die, which is one further step removed from the will to suicide. Willingness to die can come as the result of great dedication to a cause. Fighting in a war in which one believes, for example, can motivate one to the extent that he is willing to die if this is the price that is to be extracted for a much desired victory. Under these circumstances, one will place himself in a dangerous situation, hoping not to be killed but willing to die if necessity dictates. People have often been observed placing themselves in deadly peril in order to protect or rescue those who are close and precious to them.

Although there may be some sort of unconscious death wish present in such circumstances, let us here accept them at face value and focus our concern on the still more difficult situations of clear suicide, where the stated intention is to kill one's self, and the self-inflicted action produces the fatal result. Is such a death ever rational, permissible, admirable, in the best interest of the deceased, and in accordance with his own will? Or are suicidal deaths always the result of intense feelings which distort judgment? Are suicidal deaths always a tragedy, always unnecessary, or are some, as Hemingway stated, a kind of victory? Should every suicide be prevented or should some be permitted?

The Human Will

In order to discuss the possible existence of a will to suicide we must first say a few words about the nature of human will. In the days before Freud, there was scarcely a problem about human will. Will was that quality within a person which enabled him to overcome his baser impulses, wishes, and desires, and which enabled him to proceed along that life path which he had chosen. It is probably not an oversimplification to say that in those days mankind could be divided into two groups, those who were strong-willed and those who were weak-willed. Will power was a much admired virtue, and those who exercised it could do what they wished with their lives and avoid all sorts of sinful deviation. Rollo May describes it this way. "Will-power was conceived by our nineteenth century forefathers as the faculty by which they made resolutions and then purportedly directed their lives down the rational and moral road that the culture said they should go." [4]

When will is understood in these unidimensional terms, the issue of a will to suicide can be analyzed much as the early Stoics and Epicureans saw the issue. Stoicism held that man is the master of his own fate, and he must guide his life as he rationally will. He has the innate right to make whatever decision he pleases provided it is based on rationality and logical thinking. This includes the right to kill himself. Such a decision, however, should not be made out of feelings of cowardliness or a fear since these are unworthy feelings, and submission to them would mean not only destruction but defeat. Epicureanism could see the issue of will in much the same way. The purpose of life, according to the Epicureans, is enjoyment, and when life ceases to be enjoyable or pleasurable, then one has the right to end his own life. The open door of death is always available, offering comfort, and all one needs to do is to will it and it can be accomplished.

With the coming of the twentieth century, however, our understanding of human will underwent some profound changes. The greatest of these was heralded by Freud with his exploration of the unconscious. By uncovering this vast area of the human personality and discovering how a variety of wishes and drives play upon one another supplying much of the motivation for our actions, he exposed the concept of will as a superficial explanation of human behavior. The image that emerged was no longer that of man as captain of his soul and master of his fate, but rather man as a harried driver of an ancient chariot, struggling with all his might

[4] May, *Love and Will* (New York: W. W. Norton, 1969), p. 182.

to keep some modicum of control over the immense horse-power that often led him where he did not wish to go. "Man is lived by the unconscious," said Freud, making his case for scientific determinism as the only rational explanation of life. With the exception of some writings of Otto Rank the concept of human will was almost entirely dropped from the arena of psychology at Freudian conceptions came to dominate. So complete was this transformation in the general culture that people stopped seeing themselves as having a will, as having power or influence over what happens to them except insofar as they are able to understand and manipulate their own unconscious. The age of scientific determinism tended to undermine individual automony and the strength that had been known in the previous century as will. Rollo May spells out the effects of this.

> Indeed, the central core of modern man's neurosis, it may be fairly said, is the undermining of his experience of himself as responsible, the sapping of his will and ability to make decisions. The lack of will is much more than merely an ethical problem: A modern individual so often has a conviction that even if he did exert his will—or whatever illusion passes for it—his actions won't do him any good anyway. It is this inner experience of impotence, this contradiction in will which constitutes our critical problem.[5]

Lately, the concept of the will has been given renewed attention in the field of psychoanalysis. Leslie Farber defines will as "the category through which we examine that por-

[5] *Ibid.*, p. 184.

tion of our life, that is the mover of our life, in a certain direction or toward an objective in time." But, according to Farber, will is not the unidimensioned entity that nineteenth-century man thought.

He posits two distinct realms of will. The first realm is not usually available to conscious experience, although in retrospect its effects can be seen. Being unconscious it moves in a general direction rather than toward a particular object. A direction is "a way whose end cannot be known—a way open to possibility, including the possibility of failure." [6] This realm of will is free to think, to act, to speak forthrightly and responsibly without hazard. It is the expression of what the person wants, wishes, aspires to, and desires. It is will experienced as an oceanic mood.

The second realm of will is conscious, and therefore can be experienced during action. It presses toward particular objectives, rather than a general direction as in the first realm, and it can be thought of as being utilitarian in character. It is what we consciously want to do in a given situation. It is the activity which we will to perform because we desire the results that will flow from the action. Problems arise when we seek to apply the will of the second realm into areas of life that are really controlled by our will of the first realm. Farber gives some examples.

I can will knowledge but not wisdom; going to bed but not sleeping; eating but not hunger; meekness but not humility; scrupulosity but not virtue; self-assertion or bravado, but not courage; lust but not love, commiseration but not sympathy; congratulations but not admiration; religiosity but not faith;

[6] Leslie H. Farber, *The Ways of the Will* (New York: Harper & Row, 1966) , p. 9.

reading but not understanding. The list could be extended, but it must be clear when will of the second realm turns to such qualities that it seeks in its utilitarian way to capture through imitation their puppet face, the manner or style that is visible and objectives as well as available. I can will speech or silence, but not conversation.[7]

When we speak of the will to suicide and have in mind Farber's second realm of will, that which is conscious and utilitarian, there seems to be no deep conflict. That many people will die from suicidal actions in this way seems beyond question and many do so die, but whether such deaths are justifiable or rational in terms of Farber's first realm of will is where the issue really lies. If Freud is right, that the unconscious cannot know of its own death, then it would seem impossible that such a thing as a will to suicide exists. To see suicide as a protest, as a cry of desperation, as a dramatic, intense, willful expression is to say nothing more than we have said earlier, but to understand suicide in terms of the primary realm of will, as a deliberate movement in the direction of death and nonexistence, as the ultimate contradiction of everything we understand that phase of will to be, seems to be an impossible situation.

There is a serious question about whether one can even conceptualize his own nonexistence, let alone will it. Even in times of intense despair it seems as though the very quality of despair includes a taking of one's own will seriously, which is, in a sense, an affirmation, not a rejection of it. Yet when we turn to case material we are impressed with the apparent rationality of some suicide decisions. Take for example, a recent newspaper article.

[7] *Ibid.*, p. 15.

MONTCLAIR, N.J. (UPI) —Dr. _____ knew that neither he nor his wife had long to live. He was 79, and suffering from emphysema. She was 78 and stricken with cancer of the throat.

When they died there would be no one in the family to care for their son, a mongoloid who had to be tied to a chair to be fed and tied in his bed at night.

So _____, a pioneer in X-ray treatment for cancer with a practice decided to act "for mercy."

_____ was found dead of a gunshot wound Sunday by a family nurse, _____. Police, called to the house by _____, discovered the bodies of Mrs. _____ and the son, _____ 49, in a second-floor bedroom.

Police said the mother and son were shot in the back Saturday night with a .38-caliber revolver as Mrs. _____ fed her son.

Early Sunday morning, after signing a one-page suicide note, _____ shot himself in the mouth with the same gun.

Detective Capt. _____, who led the investigation into the case, disclosed the circumstances Monday. He said _____ wrote in the note the killings were "for Mercy."

The decision to suicide, even to homicide in this instance, although tragic, will be judged by some as rational, even noble, in the light of possible alternatives.

Conclusions

To pass final philosophic judgment on such an action one must appeal to some absolute system of values by which such judgment can be defined. As we saw in the last chapter, history has no shortage of such systems and one can select the position he wishes. The following chart can serve as a summary of the wide variety of attitudes toward the value of suicide:

A. Suicide Is Unequivocally Wrong

1. Suicide is wrong because it does violence to the dignity of human life. It is against basic human nature. Every human life is sacred and should be preserved at all cost (Kant).

2. Suicide is bad because it represents a crime against the state. Man is primarily a social being and is the property of the state, and no one has any right to deprive the state of its property (Aristotle).

3. Suicide is bad because it represents an oversimplified response to a complex and necessarily ambivalent situation (dynamic psychology).

4. Suicide is bad because it is an irrevocable act which denies future opportunity for learning or for growth (self-actualization).

5. Suicide is bad because it usurps God's perogative to give and to take away human life (theism).

6. Suicide is bad because it is unnatural. Man being the only animal who commits suicide, he thus does violence to the natural order of things (naturalism).

7. Suicide is homicide and this is forbidden (Augustine).

8. Suicide adversely affects the survivors, both immediate family and the general community (organismic theorists).

B. Suicide Is Permissible under Certain Extreme Conditions

1. Suicide is wrong because it represents rebellion against the gods, and is unworthy for the human soul. There are extreme cases, however, when the gods may approve of suicidal actions (Socrates).

2. Suicide is permissible when in the individual's view of things the alternatives are unbearable. An example is extreme and incurable physical pain (Plato).

C. *Suicide Is Not a Moral or Ethical Issue*

1. Suicide is a phenomenon of life which is subject to study in the same way that any other phenomenon of life should be studied (scientific).

2. Suicide represents neither a morally good nor a morally bad action and is essentially an action that takes place beyond the realm of reason. Man, when he is in touch with spirits of another region, moves by motivations which are unintelligible to the rational mind. Suicide may be an expression of this (mysticism).

3. Suicide is a morally neutral act in that every man has a free will and has the right, and indeed the duty, to move and act according to that will to make whatever disposition of his life he wishes, provided it does not do extreme violence to another person's free will (Hume).

D. *Suicide Is a Positive Response to Certain Conditions*

1. The purpose of life is the enjoyment of it, and when life ceases to be enjoyable or pleasurable, one has the right to end his life. The open door of death is always available, offering comfort (Epicureanism).

2. Man is the master of his own fate and must guide his life as he rationally will. He has the innate right to make whatever decision he pleases, provided it is based on rational and logical thinking. This includes the right to kill himself. Such a decision, however,

should not be made out of feelings of cowardliness or fear, since these are unworthy feelings (Stoicism).

3. There are certain times in life when death is less an evil than dishonor, when the preference should be for destruction rather than defeat (Hemingway).

4. Some suicides are demanded by society as a way of dispensing justice. For example, in some tribes the breaking of the incest taboo demands that the person leave the tribe and kill himself so that justice is restored (tribal law).

5. Suicide is a permissible act when it is performed for some great purpose that transcends the value of the human life. Examples are the self-immolations in the cause of peace (social martyrdom).

E. Suicide Has Intrinsic Positive Value

1. The important thing in life is man's ability to affirm himself and to make his own decisions. Sometimes he may decide upon suicide and such a decision may be an affirmation of his soul, in which case it is to his own fulfillment for him to carry through this action and it would be morally wrong for anyone to interfere with this decision (Hillman).

2. Suicide is sometimes a way to save face, as in the case of *hara-kiri,* after the individual has lost his honor (Oriental tradition).

3. Suicide has positive value when it provides the means by which a person can enter a meaningful afterlife which he desires (Cyprian, Tertullian).

4. Suicide is a way to embrace a personified and eroticized death. Examples are in some poetical ex-

pressions of the beauty and the seductiveness of death (the Harlequin) .

5. Suicide has positive value because it is a way in which one can be immediately reunited with valued ancestors and with loved ones (Hindu suttee) .

To try to make the judgment that suicide is right or wrong, rational or irrational, sinful or sacrificial is probably after all a meaningless task. The problem lies in the assumption that the answer can be absolute. This assumption leads us into all the problems that any absolute legalistic system entails such as: 1) What are the specific criteria? 2) Who is to make the judgment? 3) Who will judge the judge and by what criteria? And so it goes around again.

Such questions can, it seems to me, better be discussed in terms of a continuum. Some suicides appear to us as more rational or justified than others; we are more offended by certain suicides than we are by others.

The death of the aging immigrant, Nicholas Z., for example appears much less tragic to most of us than that of a productive forty-five-year-old male with a family to support. The suicide of almost any adolescent offends the community deeply and usually receives newspaper space whereas the common suicidal deaths of the elderly are ignored.

Is there such a thing as an acceptable suicide? What is often thought of as being a philosophical question appears to this author as being basically an ethical one, better phrased. Is there such a thing as a suicide which is acceptable *to me?* Can I ever walk away and say, "It's your decision"? Probably not, but the issue arises in determining how hard I will try to prevent the act.

We have tried to stress the importance of understanding

the effects of ambivalence and depression in the suicide person. To be ethical, the clinician must search himself with the same deep-probing evaluation. Is depression or fatigue leading him to stop trying and to rationalize the suicide as acceptable? Is his own ambivalence toward the suicidal person resulting in mixed communication and destructive permissiveness? That there is some will to suicide seems clear. At least twenty-five thousand people a year submit to it. The will to life, however, is also present and the clinician's task is to support it and foster it however he can. He is ethical and responsible when he, listening to his own dynamics and feelings can respond affirmatively and firmly to another's cry for help, or knowing he is unable to rsepond, helps find someone who can.

Chapter 7
Religion and Suicide

The Resources of Religion

More and more, professionals dealing with the suicidal patient are becoming aware of the necessity for leading the patient to an affirmative belief in something of value. Elsa Whalley, for example, holds that the thing of value is Reality, which she defines as being, "the process of growth which constitutes the living universe of which we are a part.[1] She would convince the patient that he suffers from a deadly myopia and that he ought to believe in and place a high value on life.

Experience indicates, however, that suicidal patients are not easily convinced of anything. They will resist any value structure being imposed on them, reacting instead to their own inner world and manifesting great suspicion of any influences.

At least one study has indicated how important religious beliefs appear to be more the product of the home environ-

[1] Elsa Whalley, "Patient and Therapist Values and the Suicide Threat" (manuscript, 1963), p. 3.

ment than of formal religious education.[2] The experiences which the child has with his mother and father appear to be closely related to his present attitudes toward God and to the nature of the universe in which he lives. If organized religion is to effect meaningful changes in the belief-structure of the suicidal person, it must first take seriously the deep roots of his present operational beliefs.

Trust

Religious belief involves the ability of the person to trust, and this appears to be one of the basic difficulties with which the suicidal person has to struggle. To him, the universe cannot be trusted, God cannot be trusted, helping persons cannot be trusted. He cannot even trust himself to continue to want to live.

According to Erikson, the establishment of what he calls "basic trust" is the first task that the child undertakes, and it relates to his conception of the world and of himself. "Basic trust . . . is an attitude toward oneself and the world derived from the experiences of the first year of life. By 'trust' I mean what is commonly implied in reasonable trustfulness as far as others are concerned, and a simple sense of trustworthiness as far as oneself is concerned." [3]

The relationships and experiences that are a part of the first year of life—particularly the relationship to the mother —represent the first crucial lessons the child learns about the world and about himself. This first year, Erikson points out, is basically an "incorporative" experience. The child incorporates a variety of experiences through all of his

[2] Paul W. Pretzel, "Suicide and Religion" (Th.D. diss., Claremont School of Theology, California, 1966).

[3] Erik H. Erikson, *Identity and the Life Cycle*, Psychological Issues Volume (New York: International Universities Press, 1959), p. 56.

senses. He learns that the world is both trustworthy and untrustworthy, as some of his needs are being met and others are being delayed. He is being cared for enough to permit him to survive in a relatively healthy way, but this survival is marked by frequent frustration and delay.

The lessons that the child learns in this first period of life are important, not only in his basic concept of the outside world, but also in his basic concept of himself. "The general state of trust, furthermore, implies not only that one has learned to rely on the sameness and continuity of the outer providers but also that one may trust oneself and the capacity of one's own organs to cope with urges; that one is able to consider oneself trustworthy enough so that the provider will not need to be on guard or to leave." [4]

But the problem of basic trust is never entirely solved in early childhood. It remains an issue for all men throughout their lives. Later experiences can either enhance or diminish the quality of trust that the infant has received. Erikson sees religion as being one important way in which the basic trust of a person can be reinforced. "All religions have in common the periodical childhood surrender to a Provider or providers who dispense earthly fortune as well as spiritual health." The value of a sustaining religious belief, according to Erikson, should be obvious to everyone who works professionally with people. "The psychotherapist cannot avoid observing that there are millions of people who really cannot afford to be without religion." These people need the succor and nourishment that religion gives them, the strengthening of their basic trust in the world, in

[4] *Ibid.*, p. 61.

the universe, and in themselves. But religion is not the only source of these benefits. "On the other hand, there are millions who seem to derive faith from other than religious dogmas, that is, from fellowships, productive work, social action, scientific pursuit and artistic creation." Yet, even with this understanding, Erikson stresses "that religion through the centuries has served to restore a sense of trust at regular intervals in the form of faith while giving tangible form to a sense of evil which it promises to ban." [5]

If one does not have such a religious faith, he must derive such basic trust from other sources. Suicidal persons have failed in this. They cannot find such support either from religion, nor have they been able to find other sources to enhance their basic trust. They have no sense of strong commitment to any cause or institution, nor are they able to form the kind of deep human relationships that are feeding and sustaining.

Even in adulthood they remain infants who cannot trust the breast to be a good one. They turn away from it in distrust and then suffer the pains of emotional starvation. They are suicidal because they cannot trust in life and so are cut off from the sources of nourishment that the world offers.

H. C. Rumke also stresses the need of human beings to be able to trust, and he identifies the sense of trust with man's religious intuition. He points out that throughout life there is much more that we do not know than that we do know. Unless we are able to act on beliefs, as distinguished from knowledge, we are paralyzed. It is only when we can act on faith that we can act at all.

Ibid., pp. 64-65.

The whole of life is based on a trustful belief. Without belief and faith in this general sense, life would be quite impossible. When we try to take our bearings in the outside world, in relation to people, to things, to the earth and the universe, and *nolens volens,* build up from it, be it ever such a vague idea, we realize what an infinitesimal sum of objective knowledge covers an abysmal ignorance, in which, nevertheless, we move about and find our way with remarkable certainty, thanks to our trust and belief.[6]

The arrestment in the ability to trust is reflected in the suicidal person's conception about the world, God, and other persons. If religion is to be offered as a help to the suicidal person, it must address itself to the individual's capacity for trusting. To demand belief in certain specific convictions which the religion holds—for example, belief in a loving God or belief in Reality—is to deny the basic problem and so to reject the individual.

Instead, religion must address itself to the task of nurturing the sense of trustfulness within the suicidal person, demonstrating to him that there are some things in life which can be trusted.

If the clergyman is one who has dealt with the suicidal person during the time of his crisis, he is in a strong position to continue in a long-term therapeutic relationship. If the clergyman is willing to do this, he may be imbued with magical powers by the patient. He will be seen as being an all-wise, all-powerful figure. If the transference does develop in this way, the suicidal person's dependency problem will become manifest, and he may want his minister to make all sorts of decisions for him. He will attempt to lean

[6] H. D. Rumke, *The Psychology of Unbelief* (New York: Sheed & Ward, 1962), p. 11.

heavily on the clergyman, as if testing to see if this man can really be trusted. He will be recreating in this relationship his early family situation. He will be seeking to find, if he can, even at this late age, some way to learn to trust, and he can do it only if he finds someone who is trustworthy. Will he receive now, from this man who saved him from death, the care and concern that he did not experience from those who first gave him life?

Recognition

Another way in which to conceptualize the spiritual need of a suicidal person is in terms of the necessity for recognition, the need to have a recognizing face close to his own. The will to live or the belief that life is worth living is not implicit in the fact that one has been born. The affirmation of one's existence—the feeling of being recognized, which is so important to our own identity—is not a function that anyone can perform for himself. It must be performed for him by others. In this connection, Erikson says:

> The self-images cultivated during all the childhood stages thus gradually prepare the sense of identity, beginning with that earliest mutual recognition of and by another face which the ethologists have made us look for in our human beginnings. Their findings, properly transposed into the human condition, may throw new light on the identity—giving power of the eyes and the face which first "recognize" you (give you your first *Ansehen*), and new light also on the infantile origin of the dreaded estrangement, the "loss of face." [7]

[7] Erikson, *Insight and Responsibility* (New York: W. W. Norton, 1964), p. 95.

The suicidal person lives an estranged life, a life that has not been recognized by someone outside of himself and larger than himself. He has not been told, in effect, "I recognize you for who you are—a living person who is essentially alive." In one study all the suicidal subjects had at least one parent who denied the child this unqualified recognition and affirmation. The sources of their lives failed to affirm their lives and endorse them. This primary parental effect was so strong that even though many of the subjects were exposed to the teachings of the Church, the basic message that "God affirms your existence" never got through. They feel that they are trespassers in the land of the living, they have never been convincingly told that they belong alive, that this is their right and their essence. They stand before life as guests who wait for the acknowledgement by the host that he sees and welcomes them. Holding the invitation in hand, they stand at the door but cannot comfortably go in and join the guests and partake of the feast until the host recognizes them and affirms that they belong.

Durkheim hinted at this basic need for recognition and affirmation when he laid stress on the importance of a person's feeling a part of an integrated society. Society says to its members, "you belong, you have a place, you can live." It is a recognition that it denies to the outsider.

Religion has the tools to provide this basic recognition, and if it uses them wisely, it can speak to the deepest needs of the suicidal person. Certain religious ceremonies such as baptism and confirmation and bar mitzvah attempt to serve this vital need. In the ceremony, the religious community confronts the fact that the person is alive and confirms it.

The community of God and God himself—the Ground of Being—recognize the person and affirm his identity.

But religion cannot accomplish this quickly, easily, or superficially. When religion addresses itself to a suicidal person, it must be prepared to take seriously the depth and complexity of the problem and be ready to minister gently, warmly, and persistently.

Religion as a Response

Historically, religion has seen the problem of suicide as part of its province of concern, because religion professes deep interest in spiritual development, and when a person is suicidal he is in a spiritual crisis of the gravest proportions. Psychology has discovered that some of the factors involved in a suicidal crisis are feelings of guilt, abandonment, anger, and hopelessness. These are some of the feelings that religion has traditionally felt called to respond to.

The suicidal act is a cry for help. It has been described as a cry directed to the significant others in the suicidal person's life sphere. But it can also be seen as a cry of spiritual desperation—a cry to God.

The theological meaning of suicide has been almost totally ignored in theoretical writings of the past. But when a person says by word or act that he prefers death to life, it is a situation that carries grave theological implications, and at the same time offers a challenge to religion to seek to understand more clearly what the ministry to such persons ought to be.

If religion is serious in its mission to seek out and save the lost, it cannot ignore the suicidal person who represents the extreme feeling of spiritual abandonment. It cannot fail to accept the challenge to enter the dark forbidding world of the person seeking his own death. This is a valley where the shadow is dark and frightening indeed, but if the major religious institutions of our culture are to be true to the beliefs they profess, they must not avoid the path that leads through such dangerous territory.

However, in dealing with a suicidal person from the viewpoint of religion, an important distinction must first be established. When the person is in the midst of his crisis, the initial response which religion can make will be different from that which it may make after the immediate crisis is past.

In Time of Crisis

During the crisis itself, "the principle factors are the overwhelming importance of an intolerable problem and the feelings of hopelessness and helplessness." [8] The technique for handling the suicidal person in crisis, developed by the Los Angeles Suicide Prevention Center, has been organized in six phases. These are not necessarily accomplished in this order, but all need to be dealt with.

1. The helper must attempt to establish a relationship with the suicidal person, if none is preexistent. The association should be one of mutual trust and respect and be characterized by a free flow of feelings and information. It is important that contact with the suicidal person be maintained as long as is necessary.

2. The focal problem should be identified and clarified. Frequently the suicidal person is confused and disorganized. He is experiencing chaotic feelings, and may have great

---

[8] S. M. Heilig, et. al., "Manual for Clinical Associates" (manuscript, Los Angeles Suicide Prevention Center, 1965), p. 3.

difficulty in defining precisely what the problem is. Frequently, once the problem has been identified, the patient experiences a feeling of relief and is able to place his life in better perspective.

3. The helper will try to evaluate the suicidal danger which the patient represents, so that the response will be appropriate.

4. In addition to defining the nature and the seriousness of the problem, the helper will attempt to assess the person's strengths and resources. The suicidal person often feels as though he has no assets upon which he can draw. Careful examination of his situation usually reveals resources which he had not thought of and which can make an important difference to him.

5. All the patient's resources, those within his own personality and those external to himself, should be mobilized. The helper should encourage the patient to do everything he can for himself and be willing to help with what the patient cannot manage.

6. Some therapeutic plan must be developed and implemented. It may include hospitalization, psychotherapy, family counseling, or whatever else seems appropriate and helpful. Whatever the plan, a suicidal crisis calls for action of some sort, and the helper accepts the responsibility to aid in its conception and implementation.

In recent years a movement has begun in the Church for the express purpose of seeking out and responding to persons in crisis. In 1966 an international organization was founded based on the work of Dr. Alan Walker at the Central Methodist Mission in Sydney, Australia. Known as Life Line, the movement provides twenty-four-hour crisis telephone coverage to everyone in the community. Calls are received from people in crisis and are handled by well-trained and experienced counselors.

In the United States this organization has taken the name CONTACT. An interdenominational organization, CONTACT helps church-related telephone centers become established and provides guidelines for high standards. Specifically Christian in its approach, CONTACT is to "be staffed by persons willing to engage in this service as a ministry to human need in the name of Jesus Christ, and to be nurtured and sustained in this mission by the Christian church as a community of faith." [9]

CONTACT workers are trained to handle a variety of crises, including that of suicide.

In Postcrisis Time

Once the crisis has passed, however, and the immediate danger of suicide has somewhat lessened, once the flood of feelings has abated to the point where they are more manageable, the role of the helper can change from one of crisis intervention to one of helping the person to reestablish his life. Just as the human problem of the alcoholic is not solved when he recovers from a binge, so the human problem of the suicidal person is not solved when the immediate crisis is survived. Persons who have survived one suicide attempt are likely to attempt it again at a later time unless some significant change is effected. What benefits can religion offer to affect the person to such an extent that he can be saved from a subsequent suicidal crisis?

In one study, four of five subjects were raised with some

[9] "The State of the CONTACT Teleministry Movement," Ross E. Whetstone. Address before the National Conference of CONTACT Teleministries at Newport News, Virginia, April 17, 1971.

significant contact with institutional religion, yet this exposure did not save them from being dangerously suicidal, nor did any of them move closer to their historic religious faith as a resource in their crisis.[10] This would suggest that either religion is not important as a deterrent to suicide or that the particular religions did not communicate the value that is present in their belief-systems.

This study suggests that some suicidal persons to not find symbolic actions or abstract doctrines to be helpful. They do not find prayer meaningful; forgiveness is a difficult concept for them; they do not depend on God or any "beneficient possession"; nor can they be satisfied with long-range rewards for present-day sufferings. They have little faith in an unseen, cosmic order. Sunday school and church services appear to have little effect. Efforts at preaching, administering the sacraments, leading in prayer, teaching doctrine, offering words of forgiveness, exhortation to put one's life in the hands of God, will have little positive effect.

Pastoral Opportunities

In spite of the fact that the suicidal person is usually alientated from whatever religious background he has had, it is true that organized religion has some unique opportunities to work effectively in the field of suicide prevention.

The report of the National Institute of Mental Health, *Action for Mental Health,* indicates that more people initially take their emotional problems to clergymen than to any other single professional group. This places the clergyman in a key position to detect possible suicidal danger.[11]

[10] Pretzel, "Suicide and Religion," p. 210.
[11] (New York: Basic Books, 1961), p. 103.

In addition to his contact with those who are actively seeking help, the clergyman has frequent contacts with many persons who are troubled but who have not as yet sought assistance with their problems. In his day-to-day calling and in his dealing with the members of his parish and his community, he has the opportunity to keep in touch with many different home situations. Most persons who make a suicide attempt have tried to communicate their intention to do so, although the threat is often veiled and disguised. If a clergyman is trained to read the signs and to interpret the communication that the suicidal person is attempting to make, he can often intervene in time to avert a crisis and possibly a tragedy. Suicidal situations are frequently found to have developed in families where communication is hindered and distorted, and the clergyman is often in a strong position to help the family deal more creatively with their problems.

A third opportunity for the clergyman lies in his frequent involvement with the family which is undergoing a crisis. It is common for the clergyman to be called into stressful situations, such as a death in the family or a serious illness, and it is appropriate for him to take the initiative in offering his services in these circumstances. Especially in times of loss or impending loss—times which may trigger suicidal impulses—the clergyman is often in the best position to offer lifesaving aid.

Finally, the representative of the religious community is usually in close touch with his community's social and political structure, and can speak with some influence. He can use this influence to guide his community in providing professional crisis facilities as they are needed.

Planning Pastoral Therapy

Although flexibility and creativity are vital characteristics of the treatment of suicidal persons, certain general principles can be observed:

1. It is important that the present religious views which are held by the suicidal person be understood and accepted by the would-be helper. Many of the beliefs which the patient expresses are likely to be in direct contradiction to the beliefs that are held by the clergyman. The suicidal person is apt passionately to deny belief in God, in prayer, in the value of life, in the possibility of any hope. But it is important that the helper be willing and able to understand the present position of the patient and be able to accept him in his present frame of reference. The patient needs to be recognized for what he is—a person who believes certain things about himself and about life. This need for recognition has been discussed earlier and must be taken into account if the suicidal person is to be helped.

2. The pastoral counselor may then wish to evaluate the patient's religious beliefs in terms of the twelve tests of healthy religion as they have been put forth by Clinebell.[12] Such an evaluation might not be verbally expressed to the patient, but may serve the counselor by enabling him to structure the needs of the patient and indicate the direction that therapy might take. It enables the worker to clarify in his own mind as to what the problem is and facilitates the development of a therapeutic plan.

3. The basic relationship which the pastoral counselor should establish with the suicidal patient is essentially a

[12] Howard J. Clinebell, *The Mental Health Ministry of the Local Church* (Apex ed.; Nashville, Abingdon Press, 1972), pp. 30-54.

feeding relationship. The counselor must be willing to give to his patient and, at the beginning of the relationship at least, impose very few demands on him. This is not to suggest that the dependency should be encouraged to the point that the patient feels robbed of whatever dignity he has left, but sensitive clinical judgment must be exercised. Most suicidal people have a strong sense of failure and guilt, and the clergyman must be careful in what he expects of the patient.

The counselor-patient relationship, for example, should not be dependent on the patient's accepting the responsibility for any religious doctrine or practice. The patient must be left free to accept any such responsibility only when and if he feels comfortable in doing so.

The aim of the therapeutic relationship is the strengthening of the patient's sense of basic trust. He must begin by seeing the counselor as a person who is willing to give, just as the nursing mother is willing to give, asking for the time nothing in return. If the patient's sense of basic trust does begin to develop, the relationship can begin to move to mutuality. But in the beginning, the suicidal person must develop the feeling that here is one person that he can tust to care, regardless of any religious differences.

4. The pastoral counselor should be free to try unorthodox methods with his suicidal patient. Especially for the patient who has had previous exposure to religion, there is prima facie evidence that orthodox methods of religious concern did not work. There is still much to be learned in the treatment of suicidal person, and the pastoral counselor who is free to try new therapeutic methods may contribute new insights. Robert C. Murphey stresses the observation that suicide is an extreme condition and as such calls for

extreme involvement on behalf of the helper.[13] For example, the pastoral counselor may be able to mobilize his own church to provide needed support and encouragement to a suicidal person.

5. Once the therapy plan has been devised, the pastoral counselor may have to offer gentle yet persistent support for his patient to continue working. If, for example, the decision is made that the patient could be helped by involvement in some group, the counselor should be ready to handle the resistance that most suicidal persons exhibit to any long-term, intimate relationships. From time to time during the course of the relationship, the patient will express feelings of failure and hopelessness. The counselor at these times will need to play a supportive role. Just as a young child learning to walk needs courage to try again after a fall, so the suicidal patient will need courage to continue trying to reestablish himself after he suffers some failures in life. The counselor must be ready to supply the courage and the encouragement that the patient cannot muster himself.

6. The pastoral counselor must recognize that in working with suicidal persons, he is working with persons whose needs are basic and deep, going back into his earliest childhood. The counselor must be willing to demonstrate great patience, recognizing that such basic needs are not easily or quickly resolved.

7. No counselor should ever attempt to work with a seriously suicidal person alone. Professional consultation and support should always be an indispensable part of the treatment.

[13] "Office Psychotherapy with Suicidal Patients," *Voices,* (Fall 1965), 122.

The clergyman, operating in the context of his professional identity, is in the sound position to offer significant help to suicidal persons. As a figure of authority, the representative of a community, an incarnation of the life of a crucified and resurrected God, he can be a valuable transference object through which the suicidal person can begin to work through his troubles. He is in a position to speak the healing word of God which he hopes, in faith, will so work within the soul of the person who thinks of killing himself that the cry may become a cry of life instead of death. "The first cry of a newborn baby in Chicago or Zamboango, in Amsterdam or Rangoon, has the same pitch and key, each saying, "I am! I have come through! I belong! I am a member of the Family!" [14]

[14] Carl Sandburg, in Prologue to *The Family of Man*.

Selected Bibliography

A. Books

Brown, Norman O. *Life Against Death.* New York: Random House, Vintage Books, [1959].

Choron, Jacques. *Death and Western Thought.* New York: Collier, 1963.

Clinebell, Howard J. *The Mental Health Ministry of the Local Church.* Apex ed.; Nashville, Abingdon Press, 1972.

Dublin, Louis and Bunzel, Bessie. *To Be or Not To Be.* New York: Smith and Haas, 1933.

Dublin, Louis. *Suicide: A Sociological and Statistical Study,* New York: Ronald Press, 1963.

Durkheim, Emile. *Le Suicide: Etude de Sociologie.* Tr. John A. Spaulding and George Simpson. Glencoe, Ill.: Free Press, 1951.

Erikson, Erik. *Identity and the Life Cycle.* Psychological Issues. New York: International Universities Press, 1959.

————. *Insight and Responsibility.* New York: W. W. Norton, 1964.

Farber, Leslie H. *The Ways of the Will.* New York: Harper & Row, [1966].

Farberow, N. L., ed. *Taboo Topics.* New York: Atherton Press 1966.

Farberow, N. L. and Shneidman, E. S., eds. *The Cry for Help.* New York: McGraw-Hill, 1961.

Feifel, Herman, ed. *The Meaning of Death.* New York: McGraw-Hill, 1959.

Freud, Sigmund. *Civilization and Its Discontents.* Tr. James Strachey. New York: W. W. Norton, 1961.

————. *Complete Works.* Vols. IX XIV, XVII. New York: Macmillan, 1964.

————. *Beyond the Pleasure Principle.* Tr. James Strachey. New York: Bantam Books, 1959.

Gibbs, Jack. "Suicide." *In Contemporary Social Problems.* Ed. Robert K. Merton and Robert A. Nisbet. New York: Harcourt Brace Jovanovich, 1961.

Heilig. S. M. and Klugman, D. J. "The Social Worker in a Suicide Prevention Center." In *Social Work Practice,* 1963. New York: Columbia University Press, 1963. 102-12; and Parad, Howard J., ed. *Crisis Intervention: Selected Readings.* New York: Family Service Association of America, 1965, 274-83.

Henry, Andrew F. and Short, James F., Jr., *Suicide and Homocide: Some Economic, Sociological, and Psychological Aspects of Aggression.* Glencoe, Ill.: Free Press, 1954.

Hillman, James. *Suicide and the Soul.* New York: Harper & Row, 1964.

Hume, David. *An Essay on Suicide.* Yellow Springs, Ohio: Kahoe, 1929.

Jackson, Edgar. *Understanding Grief.* Nashville: Abingdon Press, 1957.

James, William. *The Will to Believe: Human Immortality.* New York: Dover Press, [1904].

Kobler, Arthur L. and Scotland, Ezra. *The End of Hope.* Glencoe, Ill.: Free Press, 1964.

May, Rollo. *Love and Will.* New York: W. W. Norton, 1969.

Meerloo, Joost. *Suicide and Mass Suicide.* New York: E. P. Dutton, 1968.

Menninger, Karl. *Love Against Hate.* New York: Harcourt Brace Jovanovich, Harvest Books, [1952].

————. *Man Against Himself.* New York: Harcourt Brace Jovanovich, Harvest Books, [1938].

Parad, Howard J., ed. *Crisis Intervention.* New York: Family Service, 1965.

Pelikan, Jaroslav. *The Shape of Death.* Nashville: Abingdon Press, 1961.

Pretzel, Paul W. "The Clergyman's Role in Crisis Counseling." In Howard J. Clinebell, ed. *Community Mental Health.* Nashville: Abingdon Press, 1970.

Shneidman, Edwin, ed. *Essays on Self-Destruction.* New York: Science House, 1967.

Shneidman, Edwin S. and Farberow, Norman, eds. *Clues to Suicide.* New York: McGraw-Hill, 1957.

Tillich, Paul. *The Courage to Be.* New Haven: Yale University Press, 1952.

Varah, Chad, ed. *The Samaritans: To Help Those Tempted to Suicide or Despair.* New York: Macmillan, 1965.

Westberg, Granger. *Good Grief*. Philadelphia: Fortress Press, 1962.
White, Robert W., ed. *The Study of Lives*. New York: Atherton Press, [1963].

B. Journal Articles

Farberow, N. L. and Shneidman, E. S. "A Study of Attempted, Threatened, and Completed Suicide." *Journal of Abnormal and Social Psychology*, L (1955), 230.

Farberow, N. L., and Palmer, Ruby. "The Nurse's Role in the Prevention of Suicide. *Nursing Forum*, III (1964), 93-103.

Farberow, N. L., Litman, R. E.; Schneidman, E. S.; Heilig, S. M. Wold, C. I.; and Kramer, Jan. "Suicide-Prevention around the Clock. *American Journal of Orthopsychiatry*, XXXVI (1966), 551-58.

Grollman, Earl A. "A Pastoral Counseling of the Potential Suicidal Person." *Pastoral Psychology*, XVI (January 1966), 18.

Grotjahn, Martin. "Ego Identity and the Fear of Death and Dying." *Journal of the Hillside Hospital*, IX (July 1960), 3.

Heilig S. S., and Farberow, N. L. "Manual for Clinical Associates." Forthcoming.

Heilig, S. M., Farberow, N. L., Litman, R. E., and Shneidman, E. S. "The Role of Non-professional Volunteers in a Suicide Prevention Center." *Community Mental Health Journal*, forthcoming.

Klugman, D. J., Litman, R. E., and Wold, C. I. "Suicide: Answering the Cry for Help. *Social Work*, X (1965), 43-50.

Lindemann, Erich. "Symptomology and Management of Acute Grief." *Pastoral Psychology*, XIV (September 1963), 8-18.

Litman, R. E. "Acutely Suicidal Patients: Management in General Medical Practice." *California Medicine*. CV (1966), 168-74.

———. "Emergency Response to Potential Suicide." *Journal of The Michigan State Medical Society* LXII (1963), 68-72.

———. "Immobolization Response to Suicidal Behavior." *Archives of General Psychiatry*, XI (1964), 282-85.

———. "When Patients Commit Suicide." *American Journal of Psychotherapy*, XIX (1965), 19, 570-76.

Murphey, Robert C. "Office Psychotherapy with Suicidal Patients." *Voices*, I (Fall 1965), 122.

Pretzel, Paul W. "The Role of the Clergyman in Suicide Prevention." *Pastoral Psychology*, XXI (April 1970).

———. "Suicide and Religion: A Preliminary Study." Th.D. diss. Claremont School of Theology, 1966.

Tabachnick, Norman. "Counter-Transference in Suicidal Attempts." *Archives of General Psychiatry,* IV (1961), 158-261.

————. "Interpersonal Relations in Suicide Attempts." *Archives of General Psychiatry, III* (1961), 16-21.

————. "Suicide and the Clergy." *Bulletin, The Council for Social Service* (Published by the Anglican Church of Canada, Toronto), 1966, *194,* 1-6.

Tabachnick, N. D. and Klugman, D. J. "No Name: A Study of Anonymous Suicidal Telephone Calls." *Psychiatry* XXVIII (1965), 79-87.

Whalley, Elsa A. "Patient and Therapist Values and the Suicide Threat." Paper presented before the American Psychological Association, August 29, 1963.

Zilboorg, Gregory. "Differential Diagnostic Types of Suicide." *Archives of Neurology and Psychology,* XXXV (1936), 270.

————. "Suicide Among Civilized and Primitive Races." *American Journal of Psychology,* XCII (1936), 1347.

————. "Considerations on Suicide with Particular Reference to That of the Young." *American Journal of Orthopsychology,* VIII (1937), 15.

Index

Case Illustrations

About the Author

Paul W. Pretzel is a practicing clinical psychologist in Los Angeles, California. He served as staff psychologist and co-director of Clinical Services at the Suicide Prevention Center in Los Angeles for five years.

In addition to his private practice, he is assistant professor in the Psychology Department of California State College in Los Angeles and serves as Mental Health Consultant of that city. He also serves on the Board of Directors of CONTACT, Teleministry, Inc.

Dr. Pretzel received his TH.D. degree in 1966 from the School of Theology in Claremont, California.